THE CULTURE OF
SUCCESS

**10 NATURAL LAWS FOR CREATING THE PLACE
WHERE EVERYONE WANTS TO WORK**

By
Steven J. Anderson

Published in 2015 by The Yes Press

Library of Congress Cataloging-in-Publication Data
1. Anderson, Steven J. 2. Management. I. Title

ISBN 978-1-4951-2923-0
Printed in the United States of America
The Yes Press • Dallas, Texas
2nd Printing, 2017

The Culture of Success: 10 Natural Laws for Creating the
Place Where Everyone Wants to Work / Steven J. Anderson

Cover design by Jesse Brand
Book designed by Ed Brinton
Book edited by Mike Steere

*To Arthur S. Anderson who gave me
my first "ticket" to a Culture of Success.*

On a Culture of Success...

"An organization that endures is an organization that creates and maintains a *culture of success*. The foundation for Henry Schein's culture of success is the concept of 'doing well by doing good' – that our company thrives when we make a meaningful contribution to society. This is certainly a philosophy that we share with Crown Council /Smile for Life, and one of the reasons we are so proud to be your partner."

—Stanley Bergman, Chairman of the Board and CEO, Henry Schein

"A worthwhile practice and a fulfilling life are built on a solid vision and the principles of a *Culture of Success*."

—Dr. Roy Hammond, Founder, Learning Curves and Smiles for Hope Foundation

"Business financial success is built on a solid business model that incorporates the natural laws of a *Culture of Success*."

—Dan Wicker, CPA, Partner, Cain Watters and Associates

"A company that serves the market best is a company built on a *Culture of Success*."

—Dan Fischer, Founder and President, Ultradent Products, Inc.

"The best employers where everyone loves to work follow the principles of a *Culture of Success*."

—Barbara Freet, Founder, President/CEO, Human Resource Advisors

"A great image in the on-line virtual world starts with creating a Culture of Success in the office every day."

—Jack Hadley, Founding Partner, My Social Practice

CONTENTS

THE LAW OF EMOTION

NATURAL LAW:
People primarily make decisions emotionally, then justify their decisions with logic.

A CULTURE CRISIS (True Story)

The request came from a partner in a business that wanted to increase sales. The problem, he said, was the team. They just weren't producing, and he wanted us to implement our systems to get them performing at peak levels. We worked out a plan for an initial analysis and a tentative timeline for on-site training to begin a few weeks out.

Then I got a 911 call from the client asking for the first on-site meeting to be moved up because of a crisis involving the partners. It just so happened my short-term schedule could be re-arranged. "Hold on," I told him, "Help is on the way." I had no doubt that we could help. After all, success in any organization starts at the top. If any progress were to be made in this situation, it had to start with the leadership.

I haven't seen many who needed our help quite so badly as the business partners I sat down with a few days later. These were smart, highly educated individuals with a multi-million dollar company built on their knowledge and technical skills, but something was making an absolute mess out of them. They couldn't even look at each other, and speaking was painfully difficult. If the atmosphere of a closed-door meeting could be toxic – literally, not figuratively – we all would have been dead within seconds.

Like a physician treating an infected wound, I began the process of getting all the issues out on the table and exposing them to the sunlight and oxygen of open, clear communication. It became perfectly understandable why people had a hard time speaking of the root cause of their problems – an extramarital affair between one of the partners and an employee that had become common knowledge throughout the company. Even in private, the senior partner couldn't bring himself to take his junior colleague to task. The illicit lovers, meanwhile, were sure their misbehavior was "private" and nobody's business but their own.

This was destructive self-delusion. What they did precipitated a complete disintegration of trust at all levels among the partners and their employees. The issue also became an extremely costly distraction that made it difficult for team members to focus on their work. Performance at every level suffered. Customers felt it, and bottom line results showed it. At what was once a good place to work, things had gone wrong. Bad behavior had corrupted the entire company's culture.

CULTURE DEFINED

Culture, in the sense we use it, is an all-important, all-embracing concept in the daily life and performance of workplaces. It is also the subject of this book.

> Culture is a combination of the beliefs, values, attitudes and resulting behaviors in an organization. It embraces everything that affects what it's like to work in a given environment. It manifests itself most in the group's behavior and communication habits.

Absolutely every organization, which is to say every shared endeavor involving more than one person, has a culture, which is the DNA of the organization. Culture happens no matter what, either by design or by default. It usually happens the wrong way, by default, because leadership generally doesn't think about it, much less talk about it. The only time it's discussed is in a crisis, like the crisis of the aforementioned partnership in deep distress.

This book is all about things that the vast majority of people in business don't talk about – things unspoken, unwritten, not understood or even acknowledged. Our purpose is to get you thinking and talking about how to create a happy, thriving workplace where both your people and clientele want to be.

> You have in your hand a playbook for creating and maintaining a Culture by Design right for your organization – your Culture of Success.

THE FAULTS OF DEFAULT

The office affair is, I admit, a lurid beginning, but it's a vivid example of what can happen when a culture develops by accident with no discipline or direction. You can see in this story, writ large, the symptoms of Culture by Default.

Symptom #1: Misdirected Focus

In our case history of the troubled partnership, the team got so caught-up in the real-life soap opera in their midst that they lost proper focus and wasted enormous amounts of valuable time buzzing about the latest episode, to the point that work became more like a distraction from their daily entertainment.

Symptom #2: Background Noise

The office-wide buzz added to what I call background noise, which is ambient input that gives members of the team something to think and talk about that is not on target with the organizational goals. Think about trying to relax and delve into a good book or listen to favorite music, but being unable to do so because the surrounding chaos destroys your focus. That's what background noise does to a team's productive efforts. There's always a sound track running in the background – not always audible but setting the tone nevertheless. And it doesn't have to be noise. In a Culture of Success, which by definition is a Culture by Design, there's background harmony, which contributes to good results and a sense of well-being for all. As anybody who has made good music in a group will tell you, the creation of harmonious sound is deeply fulfilling. The same is true for working in harmony.

Symptom #3: Insecurity

In our case history, the background noise did more than just waste time and interfere with focus. In that noise were very troubling messages that undermined the sense of security that is foundational to a positive culture. People come to work with deep, subconscious needs, asking two big questions that relate to feelings of security:

Will I make it? This is about economic survival and keeping a job to make a living; it depends on the survival not just of the individual but of the organization.

Is this, my workplace, a safe place to be or am I emotionally at risk?

Symptom #4: Distrust

The affair – a breach of a sacred trust – made all relationships feel unreliable. And illicit management/employee romance can involve predation and misuse of power. On so many levels, the situation made the workplace a minefield. Employees even had to stress out about how to react in casual conversations: Should I laugh along with others? Or do I trust my teammates enough to say that I really believe it's shameful and tell them we really ought to regain our focus and get back to work, even if certain people would rather gossip?

Symptom #5: Complicity in Corruption

There are no innocent bystanders in culture going wrong. If you're part of it, you tacitly endorse the causal misbehavior and aid and abet it, even if the behavior in question appalls you. In our case study culture, a new woman employee was hired. Team members asked each other "Will she be the next one?" but could not warn the woman that anything was amiss during the hiring process. Thus, they were placed in an impossible situation and unwillingly covered up the leader's misdeeds.

Symptom #6: "It's Nobody's Business"

The partner cheating on his spouse deceived himself by believing he could do whatever he wanted on his own time and it would have no impact on others around him. In a Culture by Default, there is a mistaken belief that an individual can be one person at work and an entirely different person away from work. But there's always spillover, and it leads to trouble.

Symptom #7: Silent Partnership

Unwillingness to confront the cheater, on the part of his fellow partners, one of whom actually outranked him, was due in part to self-doubt – "What right do I have to call him out when I'm not perfect either?" The long-term result of that sort of thinking is a silent, unwritten contract among peers that "I won't call you out on your misbehavior, if you don't call me out on mine." This is worse than silence – it's a license to misbehave.

Symptom #8: Dread

The universal symptom of a Culture by Default, is dreading going to work. The feeling comes not from the nature of the work, but from the cultural environment in which the work must be done. If you don't like being with those you work with, it's very difficult to focus on what your work requires of you and find enjoyment in it.

The case study, while extreme, highlights symptoms that may be more subtle in your workplace. But if you can relate to any of them, it is time to get to work creating, by design, your Culture of Success.

UNIVERSAL DESIRE

Everybody wants a great place to work, but few people realize the work this takes. Culture is constantly under attack from perfectly natural forces that can cause it to unravel. Because of this, a Culture of Success is the product of consistent, systematic, disciplined effort that is unceasing.

This desire for a great workplace affects those outside your organization and goes straight to the bottom line because of the Natural Law for which this chapter is entitled: The Law of Emotion, stating that people primarily make decisions emotionally.

People outside an organization are remarkably attuned to the culture within. They'll run from an unhappy company, often without knowing why. Then they will justify the emotion-driven decision not to buy whatever you're selling the same way they would justify saying "Yes" – by retroactive rationalizing so the decision seems perfectly logical. "The price seems a little high." "I'm very busy, let me think about it." "I'm going to need some more input." "I'll let you know." These can all be reactions to dysfunctional company culture.

We would like to believe otherwise, that things in business are predictable and manageable, fact-driven and subject to logical analysis. But it just isn't so. If your people are happy in their work, your clients will be happy dealing with them. If they're miserable, your clients will know it and shy away, which is exactly what happened in the dysfunctional culture in our case study.

Think about it. Go back to the list of symptoms of a dysfunctional Culture by Default. Would you want to deal with people who are distracted, mistrustful, ashamed of goings-on in their midst they can't talk about and who generally dread where they work? No, you wouldn't. Even if the people made good-faith efforts, their misery would be, on some level, communicated to you. You'd feel it, and you wouldn't want to spend enough time with them to get to "Yes."

Everyone has had this kind of experience: You like the product, the deal is good, the geography is convenient, but something about the company selling the product just seems off.

And you walk.

By contrast, people run to places where members of the workplace team love what they do.

Just recently, I witnessed the power of the Law of Emotion in a client company of ours. It's a dental practice, which is a good model for 21st century entrepreneurial ventures – a startup with potentially high earnings built on salable technical skill. This practice was especially well run with a great culture. One afternoon the Appointment Coordinator took a call from a new patient eager to schedule an appointment, then asked the patient, as we trained her to, "Whom can we thank for referring you to us?" The new patient named another new patient who had called in that morning. Surprisingly, that person had never been in the waiting room, never met the team and dentist or experienced actual dental care, but she was so delighted with the vibe she picked up over the phone that she recommended the practice to her friend. Would that same Appointment Coordinator have been able to work the same phone magic in a bad office culture? It is highly unlikely because toxicity inevitably leaks out of an organization to the detriment of client relations.

Even in companies with little or no person-to-person client contact, such as some manufacturing, internet, and software businesses, success depends on culture every bit as much. A Culture of Success will inspire creativity, innovation, motivation, and team loyalty, which ultimately affect the quality of the product or service delivered and the company's performance. Again, culture goes straight to the bottom line.

NO, CUSTOMERS DO NOT COME FIRST

They can't, for two reasons:

1) The Law of Emotion.
2) The pre-eminence of workplace culture in how the Law affects your clientele.

If you want the customers to buy and repeat and refer – the pillars of stability and growth – you must put your own people first and keep them there, front and center. As the Prophet Isaiah said, "Set your own house in order."

Here in Texas, there's a very earthy, natural example of how it all works. Fresh garden-grown tomatoes here are an absolute delight. Even before they're ready to pick and eat, it's good to see them growing on a healthy vine. And in Texas, if you prepare the soil and are mindful of growing conditions, you can grow really nice tomatoes. Those are pretty big "ifs" though. Nothing good is going to grow in poor soil, so you have to add what your ground lacks. Because tomato plants are needy little things, you have to keep adding. And you must deal with absolute drop-dead limiting factors such as the month of July, when a tomato plant out in the open is doomed – you might as well put it in an oven. On the other hand, you can grow it in a greenhouse under controlled conditions so it gives you what you want exactly when you want it.

What if you were in the tomato-growing business? Would any amount of customer relations training and initiatives really matter if you did not create and maintain good growing conditions? Of course not, because you wouldn't have anything that people wanted.

Whatever your business, you're figuratively growing and selling some kind of tomato, the best of which never grow by accident. Your soil, your water and your climate is your culture. You've got to monitor it and take care of it all the time to keep your people fulfilled and motivated and doing their best. In a Culture by Default, you put your people in an unmonitored, uncontrolled environment. They might not die like the poor tomato plant out in July, but it's less likely that they'll love their job, work in harmony with teammates, and do their best.

It takes effort to create a Culture by Design, and the initial effort is only the beginning. You've got to monitor culture and keep it right. This is more work than most people imagine, but it's self-rewarding for you and your people and it pays off in the marketplace.

AUTHOR'S NOTE: THE LAW OF LAWS

This chapter and the nine that follow take their titles from principles of human interaction and motivation so immutable and universal that they are Natural Laws. They're the interpersonal, organizational counterparts to the Laws of Thermodynamics in physical science and such biological laws as ontogeny recapitulates phylogeny. Like the scientific laws, the human Natural Laws explain happenings that would otherwise seem mysterious and random. Knowing our Laws gives a measure of predictability and even control over the interactions and behavior of other people.

A CAUTION: Like Newton's Law of Gravity, for instance, our Natural Laws can't be broken – but try to live outside them, and they will break you.

Think, Do –

❏ **1)** Is yours a Culture by Design or Culture by Default?

❏ **2)** To what degree are the symptoms of a Culture of Default, as enumerated in this chapter, present?

❏ **3)** Are you ready to do what it takes to create a Culture of Success?

❏ **4)** If so, read on...

MISSION — What we are trying to accomplish.

VISION — Where we are going.

CULTURE — How we treat each other on our shared journey. What it's really like to be one of us.

THE LAW OF SUCCESS

NATURAL LAW:
Success is the progressive realization of a worthy ideal.

SUCCESS DEFINED

You never know when a life-changing event is about to happen, as I assuredly did not during summer vacation when I was 12 years old. The catalyst for change was my father, who remains an inspiration and role model. One day Dad came home from work and said he had a ticket to a program that featured the top motivational speakers of the day. He didn't expect me to be interested, but I surprised him by jumping at the opportunity. The next morning off I went, pedaling across the city on the same bike I rode on my paper route, which was one of my prized possessions. I was so proud of that purple bike, with its banana seat and tall ape hanger handle bars.

While kids' fads and the wisdom of allowing a 12-year-old to take off like that on their own have changed since the late 1970's, one thing has not changed, nor will it, and that is wisdom based on life's great, ineluctable truths. And that's exactly what I was pedaling toward.

After arriving at my destination, a big indoor arena, I parked my bike, locked it, and joined a crowd where I must have stuck out like a sore thumb – one lone kid in t-shirt and shorts among thousands of grown-ups in business suits. But no one was more intent than I was. *When the student is ready, the teacher appears*, one of my mentors used to say. I must have been good and ready, because at that program I learned from luminaries that included Paul Harvey, Art Linkletter, and Earl Nightingale, who were wonderful speakers with great, inspirational things to say. The event ran for three days, and I sat through each day's sessions and took notes, which I still have. I can still recite some of the most memorable pearls from the speakers. One is a foundation of this book, so ringingly true I call it a Natural Law. To save you the trouble of going back to the beginning of the chapter, I'll repeat the Law of Success:

> Success is the progressive realization of a worthy ideal.

These are the exact words spoken by Earl Nightingale, the father of modern self-help and motivation. He changed the lives of many millions of people with the powerful thoughts expressed in his prolific writings and spoken on his national program and best-selling recordings. I highly recommend taking a minute to get on the internet and stream an audio or video clip of this late, great master motivator. The man's voice and presence are still amazing. You can imagine how mesmerizing he was in person.

But it's the meaning that makes these particular words about success immortal.

SUCCESS DIFFERENTIATED

Our popular culture confuses Success with putting points on the board and coming out on top in business, sports, or any other endeavor where results can be scored. The whole point is supposedly to out-perform the competition and/or meet one's own projected results and pre-determined goals. Such measurable achievement is, in fact, a vital component of Success. After all, you can't succeed in business if you don't survive financially, and to do that you have to make your numbers. And a sense of achievement and accomplishment is part of the intangible benefits – emotional income, I call it – that is the richest reward of true Success. But this kind of Success is so big and all-embracing that there is no metric for it. If you're talking numbers – profits, percentage increases, market share, competitive rankings, etc. – you are *not* talking about Success in the best sense, as Earl Nightingale expressed.

Nor does Success mean reaching pre-determined goals through achievement or accomplishment. Goals are destinations at which you arrive, and when you do it's a cause for celebration and setting new, more challenging goals. But you never arrive at Success, which is open-ended, a never-ending journey, a lifetime quest. **What really defines you and your Success, is how you and your team make that journey.**

- Success is about **who** not what, people not things – who you are and who the people you work with are, individually and as a team.

- Success is about **where** – where you are going together, and how you're going. Not in terms of short-term, intermediary destinations and goals but your ultimate direction.

- The direction is toward a **worthy ideal** – a standard that you and your team continually strive to live up to.

- Accomplishment is about the **doing** – Success is about **being**.

Most people don't differentiate between tangible achievements and accomplishments and the intangibles, which are more important in creating a positive culture that makes your work environment a place where everyone wants to be.

THE REWARD OF SUCCESS...

The reward of success is fulfillment. You and your team can reap the reward continually, all along the way.

THE WORTHY IDEAL PAYS OFF

It's thoroughly, demonstrably *practical*. The worthy ideal pays off – more so over the long haul than the more narrow, driven, strictly achievement-oriented approach. Why? Because it builds inner, human capital for you and your team, and earns emotional income on a daily basis. Striving for a worthy ideal is Infinitely Sustainable.

Success at any cost is *not* Success. It leads to burnout and attrition of team members. Treat others as expendable, lose balance yourself, and the cost will bankrupt you and your people emotionally, not just at work but in all areas of life. Business will suffer, too.

On the other hand, Success that strikes a balance between a fulfilling pursuit of shared ideals and business-side achievement pays off...

- Financially
- Emotionally
- Spiritually
- Intellectually

True Success works and keeps working.

ASK YOURSELF...

At the end of the day:

- Did I do good, and not just well?
- Do I feel like a better person because of...

- The activities I engage in?
- The way I go about my work?
- The way I interact with co-workers?
- The way I deal with outside stakeholders –clients, suppliers, service providers?
- Am I better, and are the people around me better, because of what I do? Every "Yes" means more well-earned, well-deserved **Fulfillment**.

SUCCESS AND THE CULTURE CUBE

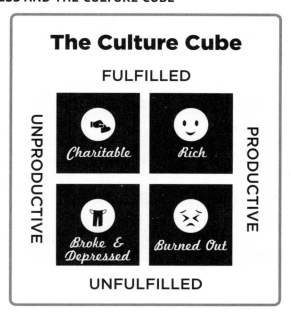

This simple schematic shows how the components of Success fit together in Organizational Culture, which balances the need to be productive and achieve results with the fulfillment from doing good for the world at large and each other. Where and how you strike the balance in your ongoing daily efforts determines your culture and your workplace environment. The cube helps you to understand both where you are and where you want to be.

THE FOUR QUADRANTS OF THE CUBE

Burned Out

Here you find results-driven, highly competitive organizations with stratospherically high expectations that they achieve. Everybody's gunning it, working 80-hour weeks, doing everything in their power to get better numbers than others. The results can look impressive, but the hallways are littered with lives sacrificed to hitting the numbers – families and personal relations neglected, mental well-being and physical health lost to stress and fatigue. People go home physically and emotionally spent and wake up and do it again, day after day. Turnover goes up with burnout. Cultures like this operate on Machiavellian principles: The end justifies the means. Win at all costs.

Charitable

First off, let me be clear: Charity – freely giving to help others, with no expectation of return – is one of the sweetest rewards of Success. Great religions deem it a sacred obligation, and the world needs a whole lot more of it. But unless you're a nonprofit distributing philanthropic dollars, you are not in business to give things away, however fulfilling that might be. Seems obvious, right? But we regularly work with clients who are not comfortable with taking money for the good things they provide, in order to make a profit and keep providing. Service and medical professionals, who sell their time to benefit others, face particular challenges in this regard. I believe it all goes back to the original motive for getting into their professions: to help people. By virtue of serving, they derive tremendous fulfillment, but then a surprising number of them feel guilty about asking to be paid.

Guilt is not what you want to feel on the accounts receivable side. And you can't sacrifice your way to Success out of misplaced guilt. We've had business owners who gave employees bonuses while they paid themselves absolutely nothing! Another kind of guilt we encounter involves under-performing staffers, whom employers sometimes keep on the payroll for years, mistakenly believing it's the right thing to do. But it's really cheating the company and the team out of what the high performers earn. In a good workplace culture, everybody wants to contribute to the bottom line. Team members understand, every bit as well as you, that work is not charity, and they want their employer to make money and stay in business.

Never forget: If you don't take care of the goose, the golden eggs will stop coming. The goose is, of course, your business and, especially, the people in it. Keep the organization happy and healthy – and profitable – the golden eggs will keep coming. Then you can donate all the extra eggs you want to the charities of your choice.

Broke and Depressed

This box is at rock bottom in both productivity and fulfillment. You're not achieving enough to get by, and you get no personal fulfillment out of what you do. Mismanagement and the wrong kind of culture can get you here, but sometimes good people in what were once good organizations end up in this square too. Cultures get turned upside-down, and companies lose their way and set goals incongruent with reality. These days we see it happen because reality itself changes.

Where technology is involved, change can be major and nearly instantaneous, making business models irrelevant. But some companies try to live in the past, doing what they've always done, expecting to achieve the way they used to. But with a declining market share, and fewer people to service, it's hard to survive and feel any fulfillment at all.

Viable, happy cultures live only in the present.

Rich

This is the square you want to be in. Creating a Culture of Success that is both high in individual and group accomplishment and across-the-board fulfillment – this is what the book in your hand is about. I use the word "Rich" in the broadest sense, meaning rich in all things, the way true multi-dimensional Success enriches you and your team. A Culture of Success makes every minute, every hour in the workplace more productive and fulfilling and improves the off-hours, too. A Culture of Success transcends the workplace and positively impacts every area of life. It's not found in only one place – you carry it with you everywhere.

To get from wherever you are now to where you want to be, in the Rich square, you must first establish your current location.

CULTURE CUBE GPS

Like a real map, the Cube is really a matrix of points on two axes, horizontal and vertical. You can plot any point by knowing where you are on each axis. Two simple 1-10 ratings get you to where you stand right now.

On a scale of 1 to 10, rate yourself on Achievement and Accomplishment. Before answering, ask yourself to what degree you are effective at predetermining results and then accomplishing them. Results are what matter here, not talk. If you nail it 8 times out of 10, give yourself an 8 (and a big pat on the back), 2 out of 10 gets a 2. The so-so number, between unacceptable and acceptable is 5. Plot your number on the horizontal axis of the Cube.

Now rate yourself on Fulfillment, 1 to 10. How you feel at the end of the day is a prime indicator. If you feel like you've been less than human with your teammates, aggressive with clients to make sales no matter what the effect on them, and generally wrung-out emotionally and ethically compromised, you're way down near 0. If, on the other hand, you feel like what you did made you and the people around you better, you're pushing 10. Plot this rating on the vertical axis of the Cube.

> Where the horizontal axis and vertical axis meet is where you are. From there you can plot the course to follow on your journey to a Culture of Success.

JOURNEYS GONE WRONG – AND RIGHT

Just about every day I pass a stone memorial that stands alongside the street I live on. It's a stark reminder of a journey gone horribly wrong and its tragic costs. In 1934, the notorious bank robbers and killers Bonnie and Clyde and their gang shot two Texas state troopers to death on that very spot. It happened on Easter Sunday, when the troopers stopped at the gang's car, which was parked along the road, to offer help.

Bonnie and Clyde were going from Point A to Point B, just like you and I and associates in our travels, and in our lifelong journeys. But those two literally left bodies all along the way, ruining untold lives, until the law caught up with them and they left their own bodies along the road. Nobody who travelled with them was better off for it.

The example seems extreme, maybe beyond extreme, but we see lesser examples of journeys gone wrong all the time. People and their organizations may not start out that way, but somehow the compass is lost and they want to get to Point B at all costs. Whatever it takes, they'll do it. Employers cease to value their own people and burn through them. The win-no-matter-what mentality infects everybody at all levels, so interactions become dishonest and mean-spirited. People lie, cheat, and steal (sometimes literally) to get what they believe they want. The whatever-it-takes culture is corrupt, top to bottom, and it breeds nothing but misery. Sometimes it leads to disaster en route, but even those who get to Point B suffer internal damage. They can't enjoy the journey because all along they feel used-up and morally spent.

A Culture of Success keeps you on track. Begin by making firm decisions about how you will treat each other and behave, and stick to those decisions. As you do so, the journey itself will make all involved better human beings, every step of the way. When you get to Point B and Point C beyond it, you and your teammates will arrive safe and sound, able to look in the mirror and feel proud of the people you see. Your vehicle on the Success Journey is your workplace, where everyone, driver or passenger, has a role in making the trip – and themselves – better. To get on-board with the right kind of culture, everyone needs to know the Rules of the Road...

Which you are about to write.

Think, Do –

❏ **1)** Where are you, as an individual, on the Culture Cube, and how do you feel about it?

❏ **2)** Is this where you want to be? If not, why not?

❏ **3)** What steps will you take to move in the right direction?

❏ **4)** Go back to the position of your organization on the Cube. Is it where you want it to be?

❏ **5)** What can you do to positively impact the organizational culture?

❏ **6)** Start taking steps in the desired direction!

THE LAW OF INTEGRITY

NATURAL LAW:
We want to be consistent with who we say we are.

MISTER M. VERSUS THE CULTURE OF CHAOS

No executive on the planet would want to be in the shoes of Mr. M, who had to turn around an organization going straight down the tubes. To do so he had to establish a Culture of Success where there was not one but two catastrophic legacy cultures.

The root cause of the mess was an old, old Culture of Tyranny. Generations of team members had labored under despots who were high-handed, arbitrary, and just plain mean, who made their authority felt through minions who were even meaner. Any wish or passing whim was law, whether or not it made sense or completely contradicted what came down from on high yesterday. Woe to anybody who didn't obey instantly and work until he or she fell over. Just look like you might question authority and you were terminated on the spot. You could be terminated just because the boss was in the mood. This went on for so long that all memory of living any other way was lost.

Then came a relocation and a new, far more enlightened regime headed by Mr. M. People celebrated their new-found freedom, but their problems were far from over because a Culture of Tyranny does damage after the actual tyranny ends. People don't know what to do with freedom, and so theirs is the Culture of Chaos. We see it happen in nations, and in companies where bosses dominate staffers to the point that they can't act on their own because they only know how to react out of fear. By the time the reign of terror ends, individuals have been devalued so long they don't value and respect each other or their group as a whole. Decency doesn't stand a chance, and people become either victims or victimizers.

By sheer will and natural-born leadership, Mr. M managed to maintain a modicum of order – but only as long as he was in the office. Every time he left, the organization unraveled to the point that survival itself was in question...

Until he came home with the solution to the organization's problems in his hands.

THE STORY PROBABLY SEEMS FAMILIAR

It's straight out of the Book of Exodus in the Old Testament, and people have been telling it for thousands of years.

Mr. M is the Biblical prophet and patriarch Moses, who led the Israelites out of Egypt where they had been held in bondage for more than 400 years by a long line of Pharaohs, Egypt's harsh and autocratic rulers. There were a huge number of liberated Israelites – over a million by some authoritative estimates – so the organizational challenges would have been immense in any circumstances. For Moses they were mind-boggling, because his people had no clue about self-determination and self-reliance, and they had to eke out their livings in The Wilderness, an unproductive desert. When Moses was called away to be with God on Mt. Sinai, things went downhill to the point that his people actually rejected God to worship an idol and generally behaved abominably.

But then Moses came down off the mountain carrying stone tablets on which a set of rules were written. Those rules became the basis of one of the world's great Cultures of Success. The Israelites got straight with their leadership, and each other, then journeyed to the Promised Land and on to major achievements and glory. But when they broke the rules, they suffered grievously. Those same rules became the basis for our civilization's moral code, ethics, civil law, and government.

There is world-changing power in The Ten Commandments.

There are also keys to understanding how to make rules for creating your own Culture of Success. By the end of this chapter you will become your own Moses and write your own

Commandments – otherwise known as a Culture Guide – so your workplace team can be productive and fulfilled.

THE ORIGINAL

Thou shalt have no other gods before me.

Thou shalt not make unto thee any graven image. (Idols)

Thou shalt not take the name of the Lord in vain.

Remember the Sabbath day, to keep it holy.

Honor thy father and thy mother.

Thou shalt not kill.

Thou shalt not commit adultery.

Thou shalt not steal.

Thou shalt not bear false witness against thy neighbor.

Thou shalt not covet.

ORGANIZATIONAL CULTURE VERSION

It's striking and significant that these fundamental guidelines from the Supreme Being define *relationships* between top leadership (God) and followers and amongst the followers and give instructions about how all involved should interact. These rules established a culture that was brand-new for the Israelites, whose culture to that point came from centuries of slavery that they desperately needed to leave behind. But the Ten Commandments also lay out basic principles for interaction and behavior within any organization. Here, by the numbers, are the commandments reinterpreted as rules for workplace culture:

Rule 1: There's one top leader in the organization. Follow her or him. Be loyal to the leader and you will be loyal to the organization.

Rule 2: Dump the old cultural junk. Don't bring the bad cultural habits from your previous workplace with you. There are new rules now, so forget the old ones and interact and behave in our new, better ways. (For the Israelites, idol worship was Egyptian religious junk).

Rule 3: Respect and honor the big boss. All the other bosses, too. Hold those up the chain of command in high esteem and act like it. Don't make of fun of them behind their backs, or do anything else in their absence that you wouldn't do in their presence. [This is, by-the-way, very sound organizational psychology. Respect for the leader breeds respect among the followers for each other. The attitude followers have about their leaders and their behavior regarding him or her, eventually becomes the attitude and behavior followers have toward each other.]

Rule 4: You shall attend and act as expected at all scheduled gatherings of our team, which are important because they strengthen commitment to our work, reinforce our core values, and remind us of who we are. Be early, and be ready to participate.

Rule 5: Show respect and deference for others' roles and areas of assigned accountability. Help them succeed by doing your best. If personal feelings get in the way, set them aside, and never walk away and let others fail.

Rule 6: Don't mess with anyone else's position in the organization and livelihood, which are strictly off limits. In workplace culture, a job is tantamount to life, and every job-holder has a unique value worthy of honor and respect. [The original Commandment, *Thou shalt not kill*, was a major cultural shift for the Children of Israel who had just escaped a culture where their lives had no value. Pharaoh and his regime killed at will.]

Rule 7: Do not violate or cause trouble in anyone else's committed relationships. And honor your own. Show respect for others' friendships, close working relationships, romances, family ties, and, above all, marriages. [Marriage vows and blood ties meant everything to a patriarchal, tribal people like the Israelites, because family was the fundamental unit of society and economic production.]

Rule 8: Don't take what belongs to the organization. You are a steward. Protect the assets with which you have been entrusted. Company assets are not yours.

Rule 9: Don't tell lies about other people or anything else. Tell the truth, because an organization that is not based on truth will fall apart. Tell the truth for your own sake, too.

Rule 10: Don't wish you had what rightfully belongs to others and resent them for having what you want. Envy is poison that destroys happiness and healthy ambition. What you really should want is to do what it takes to earn the desired attainment – promotion, Employee of the Year award, car, house with an in-ground pool, and the like. Admire the possessor and learn from his or her example.

> ### THE POSTAGE STAMP – Story and Thought Questions
>
> This was an oft-told tale in our family that involved the man in charge of a major financial institution who was one of my father's clients. One day the big boss banker saw an employee sticking a postage stamp onto an envelope. He asked the employee if that was personal mail, and if that was the bank's stamp. The employee answered 'Yes' to both questions, and was immediately told, "Gather your things and go home. You're fired." The moral of the story, from the banker's point of view, was this: No matter what the value, if you take something that belongs to the bank, you're a thief who can't be allowed to work here.
>
> Would you have fired the employee? Or felt it was fair if you got fired? If not, why not, and why is small-scale dishonesty acceptable?

MY MOSES MOMENT

The idea of creating what I now call a Culture Guide was born out of my own frustration – anger, to be honest – when nobody at the company I headed showed up on time at a scheduled morning meeting everyone knew about. I relate our situation to that of Moses and the Israelites, because I had just relocated the company to get us out from under the direct rule of our founder, who was a tyrant. The company had been built on the man's public presence and sales genius, but he was one horrible manager. He ruled by fear, and chaos followed him wherever he went. Three hundred miles away we were still in chaos – witness the nonstarter morning meeting – because people didn't know how to act in the absence of fear.

While I sat alone, anger simmering, it dawned on me that I was the one to blame, because I had not made my expectations crystal clear about meeting attendance and punctuality and a host of other things. So I ascended my own figurative Mount Sinai, thought deeply for some hours, and descended with our workplace Commandments, if you will, a rulebook for how we would agree to interact and behave in our workplace. This Culture Guide became foundational in our work together as a team, which was more productive and fulfilling because we had written rules to follow.

At the end of this chapter you'll find a slightly updated version of that original Culture Guide, which you should feel free to adapt to your situation or copy verbatim. Those we've worked with and trained say the Guide delineates the kind of workplace culture they want, and gives them a strong start on creating their own.

REMEMBER WHAT THE COMMANDMENTS WERE WRITTEN ON

It was stone, not clay tablets or papyrus, which would have been much easier for one man to carry down the mountain. Cheaper, too. But words had far greater significance carved on stone, the most durable material of the day. The message of the medium: This is very important. This is forever.

You, too, must carve your rules into stone, figuratively speaking. First, though, go over your draft version with your team, accept input and make appropriate changes, then get agreement to abide by the rules. Then it's time to carve in stone. From there on out, treat the Guide as permanent, inviolable, and important. Make sure new hires understand the rules of their new workplace culture and meet to remind the team of what is written and why it matters. This is who you are as a team.

THE MEANING OF INTEGRITY

We really do want to be consistent with who we say we are.

Integrity, in its literal, physical sense – structural integrity – refers to things put together to make a whole that won't come apart under a heavy load.

Personal and team integrity is a matter of wholeness, too. Every inconsistency – saying we're this, while acting like that – is a weak spot where culture can break and fall apart.

But to get your team on the right side of the Law of Integrity, you must first say who you are – declare it and define it with rules about how to treat each other and behave in the workplace. Then you have a cultural standard to live up to.

RULES WRITTEN IN THIN AIR

That's what you have if you just talk about expectations without putting them on paper (or the computer screen before you hit "Print"). Writing forces you and your group to think while reviewing and discussing what is written, which everybody can refer back to later. Say something without writing it, you'll have a hard time repeating your own words, which others may totally forget and misremember the point.

Unwritten rules – the only kind 98 percent of workplaces have pertaining to culture – are often just bad guesses about who expects what and bad behavior enshrined because it goes uncorrected. A Culture By Default, which sadly is typical, has a Rulebook By Default, which nobody in his or her right mind would write:

- **RULE 439:** It's okay for Lon to distract everybody and demean Charlie by snorting and rolling his eyes during Charlie's presentations at meetings, then make fun of Charlie afterward.

- **RULE 439A:** It's okay to disrespect colleagues and have fun doing it.

- **RULE 439B:** Meetings are for one-upsmanship and making other people look like idiots.

Or...

- **RULE 457:** Get things done and show off how good you are by writing emails to the boss that CC her boss and boss's boss.

- **RULE 457B:** Don't respect your boss or the chain of command.

- **RULE 457C:** Be underhanded, because that's what works.

You get the idea.

If you ever wonder if you ought to step in and correct a certain questionable behavior, make a pretend official rule that it's permissible.

By default, the craziest, counterproductive rules become part of the culture.

Leave the Culture of Default behind right now. Get out in front, write out the rules for the workplace culture you want, which your team wants at least as much as much as you do.

INTEGRITY FILLS THE EMPTY TABLES

The cuisine and service at the restaurants owned by Mr. S were famously superb. Tables were by reservation only and booked long in advance, but on a given night a restaurant might be only two-thirds full because a third of the reservations were no-shows.

Mr. S told his reservationist she needed to do something, and she ended booking calls like so: "Mr. (or Ms.) Jones, we have your reservation at such-a-date-and-time. In the unlikely event you can't honor this reservation, please call me."

No change in the no-show rate. Mr. S told the reservationist to add two words to the last sentence and see what happened. The wording was now, "In the unlikely event you can't honor this reservation, *will you* please call me?"

People said, "Yes," and the no-show rate nose-dived. Why? Because keeping a reservation and calling in any change was now more than a courtesy. It was a matter of personal integrity and conscience. It's easy to let yourself off the hook for a little thoughtlessness, especially if you're saying to yourself, "It's been a horrible, exhausting day, and I absolutely do not want to go out for dinner." But tired or not, nobody wants to be the person who makes commitments and breaks them. This isn't who we (or most of us) believe and say we are.

Think, Do –

Your turn.

❏ Write your own Culture Guide, take it to your people, fine tune it, and live by in the workplace.

Set it in stone.

For starters, use this as a model:

OUR ORGANIZATIONAL CULTURE GUIDE

Emotional & Behavioral Expectations for Our Team

Lead: BE the Organization

Wherever you are and whomever you are with, you are the organization. Live the values. Promote the vision. Be the culture by being the living example of what the organization stands for when you are with fellow team members and customers.

Live Our Culture

Team members come from varied backgrounds and experience. We value the diversity and experiences everyone brings to the organization. Put that experience to work within the defined culture of OUR organization. Leave any bad habits from previous employers behind and get fully engaged in the culture we have defined for the success of our organization and everyone in it.

Follow: Be Loyal

Every organization has leadership and organization to direct, guide, make decisions, and move things forward. People are not perfect. We all need support to do our jobs and carry out our responsibilities. Support everyone in their area of responsibility by responding, respecting, and supporting each person in their respective areas of responsibility both in and outside of his or her presence. If you can't support someone, go talk to him or her directly and get it resolved. It is unacceptable to be disloyal to any member of the team outside of his or her presence.

Respect

We always treat each other with respect. Even though we may not always agree with each other, we work out our differences and always give the benefit of the doubt to the other person. We keep all of our verbal and non-verbal communication on a respectful level and treat each other in the manner in which we would like to be treated.

Be Early

Everyone wants to work with a team where everyone can rely on each other. It starts first thing every day. That's why we all agree that, "When you're early, you're on time; when you're on time, you're late; and when you're late, you're lost."

Be Ready

In addition to being early, we are always prepared to start the day by being properly dressed, groomed and fed, with all of our work tasks in order when we start the morning meeting and at other times during the day.

Leave Your Baggage at the Door

Everything that happens in our office every day has an impact on each team member and influences how we interact with our customers. Team members bring the best of who they are to work each day by "leaving their baggage at the door" and not allowing issues in their personal life to negatively affect other team members. We consider our work environment to be "the stage" on which we perform our very best.

If You Don't Know, Don't Say

We strive to be honest in all our interactions with each other and our customers, even when it is not convenient! Occasionally, you may be asked about something you have never heard about or that you are unclear about. If in doubt, just say you don't know, but that you'll be happy to find out. Just tell the truth; that way you'll never have to try to remember what you said!

Do What You Say You'll Do

The reason our team works well together is because everyone can depend on everyone else 100%. When you commit to do something for a team member, customer, or supplier, make sure it gets done, when you promised, as you promised. If you are not sure how to do something or you know there will be things standing in the way of getting it done, say so. You always have permission up front to say you can't do it. But once you have committed, it belongs to you to get it done...so make it happen!

Be Happy to Do It!

Everyone likes to work on a team with individual members who are willing to do whatever it takes to make things happen. When asked to help or contribute, team members frequently respond by saying "Happy to do it." Having a willing attitude makes teamwork happen.

Take Problems to Their Source

When teams progress and work together, sometimes there may be differences of opinion or misunderstandings. Those can be times of great growth. If you have a problem, go to the person it involves. It is unacceptable in our office to spread gossip or talk behind a person's back. Always go back to the source of the problem and find a solution so the team can grow and move on.

Be Solution-Minded

It doesn't take much to identify a problem and tell everyone about it. It takes a great team member to identify possible solutions and act on them. In our organization we all agree that if you identify a problem, you will identify three possible solutions, one of which doesn't cost any money!

Appearance

You are the organization. Your appearance, behavior, and personal habits influence and impact your fellow teammates. Team members come to work each day properly groomed, dressed and ready to make a great first, second and never ending impression. If you wonder if something you want to wear is appropriate, just ask yourself, "What kind of impression will this leave with those I interact with today?"

Show that You Care

Other team members and customers know that we really care about them as people because we are interested in them as individuals. We put people first. Personal concern can be shown in many ways. Show them that you really care.

Acknowledge Others

Our team recognizes and acknowledges each other for contributions and performance. Take personal responsibility to thank team members who help you. Find ways to acknowledge those who do things that may otherwise go unnoticed. Congratulate customers for their accomplishments. Everyone likes to know he or she is important and appreciated. Do that for someone each day.

Follow Up

Team members form the habit of following up on actions they have initiated or things for which they have taken responsibility. For example, if you have responded to a request, following up by asking if the person got everything they needed would be appropriate. Do whatever you can to make sure there are no loose ends and that you get closure on the things you are doing.

Be Nice

Everyone likes to be treated with respect. Saying "please" and "thank you" to fellow team members as well as to our customers demonstrates an attitude of respect and cooperation.

Speak Up

We believe in involvement and participation by everyone. Speak up, give your opinion, make suggestions for new things we could be doing that will get better results with our customers. Don't wait for anyone to ask your opinion. Jump in and make a contribution!

Make it Fun!

We believe that what you do every day should be fun and exciting. Find ways each day to make our work fun, exciting and entertaining while staying "on purpose."

Keep it Clean!

We believe that people work best in a professional environment where they feel comfortable. Keeping our office clean and organized is everyone's responsibility. If you see something that needs to be picked up, do it. If you see something during the day that needs to be cleaned up in order for our customers to feel comfortable, just do it.

Change

Changes are always taking place from time to time. We consider them healthy and positive. Participate in the changes with enthusiasm. That is how we grow and learn individually and as an organization.

THE LAW OF EXAMPLE

NATURAL LAW:
What you do has far more power to influence others than just what you say.

The spirit of an organization is created from the top. If an organization is great in spirit, it is because the spirit of its top people is great. If it decays, it does so because the top rots.
– Dr. Peter Drucker

YOUR IDEAL NEW TEAM MEMBER

As any experienced manager knows, competence and professional expertise are only part – very often the lesser part – of what makes an attractive job candidate. You hire the person, not just the person's qualifications. After all, a new hire can be trained and brought up to speed on the particulars of a position, while a brilliantly qualified new addition can do more harm than good if he or she can't get along. Cultural compatibility is key, as is communicating the workplace culture and expectations so candidates know up-front what kind of a team they're joining.

First, though, you must think through and create a list of your own expectations for an ideal team member. Do it whether or not there's currently an opening. Making the list gives you a chance to eliminate, hypothetically at least, all the attributes of team members that get on your nerves. List your worst frustrations and then rule those frustrations out.

Six expectations to get you going:

- 100 percent dependable, always follows through.
- Shows up early.
- Does job with a cheerful happy-to-do-it attitude.
- Active participant at meetings, making positive contributions.
- Does more than expected.
- Helps others on the team without being asked.

Now get on your computer or an old-school piece of paper and complete your list. Think big, and don't leave anything out. After all, this is your dream team member.

REALITY CHECK

Now go through the list you just made and rate **yourself** on a scale of 1 to 5 on every expectation. Be merciless, because the more brutally honest you are with yourself, the more good this will do.

If you are honest with yourself, you will discover areas where improvement is sorely needed. Now get to work on your own deficiencies, because in matters of culture the leader leads from the front.

Lead By Example. Not by any of the old-school "I'm the Boss, and you're not!" ways of wielding power over others, which aren't really all that powerful, anyway. If you want to get your expectations out of the realm of the hypothetical into everyday working reality, you must meet or exceed your expectations for others and get the Law of Example on your side.

In truth, the Law of Example applies to everybody up and down the organizational chart and away from the workplace too, but Example is especially powerful for those in leadership roles.

Expect something of others – but the first person you should expect it of is yourself.

DO OR UNDO

The Law of Example presents this very simple choice.

Do – Live up to your expectations for others, and inspire them to do the same.

Undo – Act in ways incongruent with your expectations, and it almost doesn't matter what you say, because you're leading your people astray.

A seemingly small, thoughtless act can undermine the mightiest, written-in-stone cultural imperative, even one of the Ten Commandments. Think of a father out with his family for dinner at a fast-food restaurant. Like all good fathers, he teaches his children not to steal, a lesson they also get in religious instruction, at school, and pretty much everywhere. But at the counter he buys drinks for only two out of four kids, and lets everybody share the cups and refill from the beverage machine. Do those children see Dad cutting a little corner, saving a buck to spend on ice cream, doing something that doesn't matter because everybody else does it too? That might be what Dad tells himself, but no, that's not what they see. They see Dad steal. And the dishonesty they witness makes a more powerful statement about what's right and what's wrong than any number of words.

The example set by another father for both his family and his workplace team comes to mind. I refer to my own father. One of the most vivid memories from my teenage years involves a blizzard that hit our city long before normal snow season. We woke up on an October morning to 18 inches of snow, with streets that would remain uncleared for at least 24 hours because the municipal snow removal equipment was nowhere near ready. Most people hunkered down, except at our house. We were up before first light to shovel the drive and walks. Then, at 6:30 a.m., came a scene burned indelibly into my memory. My mother stood on our front porch, questioning the judgment of my father, who was in his car on the driveway, leaving for his office. My mother expressed herself rather forcefully. "Why," she demanded, "are you driving to work?"

I'll never forget what my father said: "If I don't, no one else will.

I'm the leader."

His leadership position was CEO of the largest advertising agency in the Western U.S. The car was a Chrysler New Yorker that was not great on snow. He went anyway, setting an example for me in my own leadership roles. His words could be a mantra for all culture-conscious leaders:

If I don't, no one will.

MIRROR CHECK

One's own reflection is a powerful inducement to peer deep within. Look yourself in the eye and reflect...

Ask yourself, **"To what degree am I living the culture I want?"**

Remember that culture will come about to the degree you live it, no more and no less.

SEE-THROUGH YOU

In matters of culture, be transparent. This means you freely and openly admit your own shortcomings vis-à-vis your stated cultural expectations.

This one is not only a reality check, but a gut check. Leaders wedded to the old school, top-down, authoritarian style of leadership will find it challenging and uncomfortable to own up to imperfections. But it's well worth it.

When cultural expectations come up in meetings and conversations – as they regularly will – jump in and tell your people that there are times when you don't measure up.

You might say, for instance, "I am fully aware that I occasionally run a little late. And that's not what we do, is it? I need to make some improvements..."

Then make a great leap farther into cultural leadership by adding this – **"Here's where I need your help."** Ask for attaboys, encouragement, and friendly reminders. We all need the help and encouragement of each other to grow and progress.

Where culture is concerned, you always want to be a player coach rather than a more remote executive who's not on the playing field. It's highly effective to lead team meetings that focus on a single expectation and cultural principle and encourage people to talk about how they can make changes and truly live the culture in this particular area. Take your turn and openly share your assessments and expectations of yourself. As I said, this can feel uncomfortable and wrong, as if you're undermining your own authority. But admitting weakness demonstrates strength and confidence that earns more respect than shows of authority and putting up barriers between you and the team. Being bossy can actually make you a less effective boss. Being transparent and making public commitments sets the example for team members to do the same.

WHY EARLY IS ON TIME

We teach the saying in every culture with which we are engaged:

When you're early, you're on time.

When you're on time, you're late.

When you're late, you're lost.

Showing up on time is impossible. You are either a little bit early or a little bit late, but never exactly on time. The typical team meeting happens with team members bustling in at the last possible minute, frazzled from rushing to beat the clock. At morning team meetings, team members can show up disheveled, carrying breakfast rolls because they didn't stop to eat. They're physically present but not settled and focused. What they are, is late, because they're not ready to work. The people who are ready show up before the appointed time, and they're dressed, made-up, fed, and 100 percent good to go when work is scheduled to begin. Starting time doesn't mean a thing unless your people are prepared to start, which means they show up early and get all the before-work distractions out of the way beforehand. Early really is right on time.

NO MORE "YES, BUT..."

The minute you hear those words in regards to culture, you know somebody's trying to get a hall pass, granting themselves some kind of exemption because they're special.

The all-time classic is this:

"Yes, but I'm the boss."

Beware, those are dangerous words. A major hazard of leadership is the temptation to believe that rules don't apply to you. Succumb to that temptation, and the culture you're building starts to unravel.

In culture, there are no exceptions, including showing up early!

THE TENURE TRAP

"Yes, but I've been here longer than anybody else."

Or any number of variations:

- "I was friends with the founder."
- "I was the one who talked them into computerizing."
- "I was number-one performer 10 years running."

Veteran employees are every bit as tempted as bosses to be selective about which rules apply to them and which don't because of their long years of service, valuable contributions, and greater wisdom than the rest of the team.

But in a Culture of Success you don't rest on your laurels, you build on them. The present and future count more than the past.

Nobody opts out.

> Experience actually brings a greater obligation to follow the rules and set an example.

A ROOKIE SHOWS THE WAY

The leader isn't the only one who has to lead by example when it comes to creating a culture of success. Rookies can do it too. The legendary pro football quarterback Joe Montana, with four Super Bowl wins and three Super Bowl Most Valuable Player awards to his credit, tells the story of one rookie player who fundamentally changed the culture of an entire team – by example.

It was the first practice of a rookie wide receiver picked up in the college draft by Joe's team, the San Francisco 49ers. The kid did the strangest thing at his first pass pattern drill. Instead of just running the pattern, making his catch, and coming back to wait his turn to do it again – like every other receiver – the rookie caught the ball, pivoted, and sprinted all the way downfield over the goal line. When his turn came again, he kept doing it, catching the ball and running all the way down the field over the goal line. Finally, one of the veteran players asked what in the world he thought he was doing.

The rookie said that back in Mississippi where he came from, he was taught that you play the way you practice. He played to make touchdowns every time he got the ball, so that is how he practiced.

At that moment, the culture of an entire NFL team underwent a fundamental change.

It turned out that the rookie, Jerry Rice, lived up to his words. He became arguably the greatest wide receiver of all time, some say the greatest NFL player, period. But successful as he was, each season he went back to train and play with the attitude of a rookie, as if he were starting all over again and had to earn his spot on the team. Even at the peak of his career, he was that same kid who showed the veteran players how to practice.

A ROOKIE FOREVER

Answer the following...

> *If you had to re-apply for your position today, would you hire yourself? Based on your performance, behavior, and attitude, do you meet your team's standards and merit your own current position?*

This brings some to a very shocking revelation – "I'm not even good enough for me to hire!"

But there's a you that *is* good enough – you when you started and strove to earn your position and keep it. Combine that energy and attitude with the knowledge and expertise you currently possess – you're a great hire, and the team is fortunate to have you.

In a Culture of Success, one of the best examples to follow is your own rookie self.

Think, Do –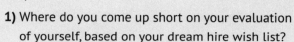

1) Where do you come up short on your evaluation of yourself, based on your dream hire wish list?

2) Write out your action plan for being a dream team leader, and get to it.

3) Be honest: What do you believe makes you the exception? That you're in charge? That you've been there longer? That you know more?

4) Make a commitment that you'll be the example of the rule, not an exception.

5) Think back to the your attitudes and actions when you were a rookie.

6) What do you need to do to reincorporate your rookie self into your current performance?

5

THE LAW OF
FREQUENCY

NATURAL LAW:
People act on what they hear and see most frequently.

ADVERTISING 101

Likely you're saying, "What's this? I'm not in advertising..."

Oh yes you are! Everyone is. And you want to be good at it. No matter who you are or what you do, you are constantly sending out messages that you hope will cause others to take some type of action. That's what advertising is. That's what advertising does.

Those who run organizations put out in-house multi-media ad campaigns to persuade their people to take desired actions. To establish and perpetuate a Culture of Success, you must promote it continually. It helps to remember three basic principles of advertising about what makes people remember messages and act on them:

PRIMACY – The *first impression* is lasting and powerful.

FREQUENCY – People respond to what they hear and see *most often*.

RECENCY – The *last thing* seen and heard sticks in the mind.

Though it shares its name with the second principle, the *Natural Law of Frequency* really combines all three, which operate together. It stands to reason that Recency requires Frequency, because the only way to ensure your message is the last one heard, is to put it out repeatedly. This accounts for the endless repetition of companies' messages. Imagine the astronomical sums GEICO has spent to plant its "Fifteen minutes can save you 15 percent or more on car insurance" mantra in the popular mind, making the message both oft-heard and likely last heard. Frequency works, or the company wouldn't pay what it costs.

But it all begins with the first principle – *Primacy*. In the realm of Culture, this means making a powerful, positive impression when you first roll out your Culture of Success for your team members.

THE ROLLOUT

Make it memorable and upbeat.

Think about having the rollout meeting catered by a local ethnic restaurant – Thai or Indian, say – with an array of foods that seem exotic but not too strange and spicy. Smaller teams might actually go to the restaurant. The food adds a festive note, and you can use it to introduce the theme of Culture. People the world over have their own distinct ways of living, which includes their own cuisines and tastes in food. Part of the cultural package includes ways of treating one another that might seem as strange or even as unacceptable to us, as our manner of interaction seems to others.

Introduce the idea that organizations like yours develop their own cultures, too, which often include things people really don't want because they don't talk about and proactively work on their culture. This meeting is about a new plan for making your team's culture better and keeping it that way.

Warm up the group with an exercise I call *Up With Which I Will Not Put*. Ask team members to write out, then share, a violation of personal boundaries or bad behavior by others so serious it would make them want to leave their jobs. The exercise becomes quite emotional for some people because it ties back to real incidents in previous workplaces that were deeply upsetting.

Establishing outside extremes of misbehavior easily transitions into talk about a good workplace atmosphere. Make the point that all of you spend as much or more time together than you do at home with your families. So it's just common sense to make work a place to which everybody can be glad to come.

Ask for a show of hands by those who want a great place to work – where you can be your best and do your best and like yourself while you're there.

Ask who would rather have a lousy work environment and say you'll be glad to help them find it!

The last line is good for a laugh. But something serious and important has happened.

You just got buy-in from the entire team.

Time to introduce your Culture Guide.

INPUT AND OWNERSHIP

Hand out copies and lead the team through the Guide point by point. Ask for comments and additions, making tweaks and additions from the team that seem appropriate. Before you leave each point and move on, be sure everybody grasps what it means and is on board with it.

In closing, ask your people, "What did we miss?" "What other things are important?" "Is there something we haven't highlighted and emphasized enough?" Ask one last time if they're all good to go with every point.

You now have clear commitments from everybody to live your new Culture of Success.

WORD OF WARNING

Creating a Culture of Success is NOT...

- An Initiative
- A Program
- A Push

Or any other name for a short-term fix that gets everybody charged-up for a little while...until they forget they ever heard of it.

> Many organizations get caught in the Flavor Of The Month trap which usually consists of the most trendy training program or organizational change effort.
> They can get some short-term results, but, inevitably, enthusiasm dies down until the next Flavor Of The Month initiative, and the one after that. So it goes, ad infinitum. This sounds pretty harmless, but it is in fact cancerous to an organization.

Training programs or initiatives, if you are not careful, can become like organization drug addiction. In order to keep the troops upbeat and motivated, you give them a quick "hit" in order to produce a "high" of productivity only to find that you have to give them another hit with another program to keep them "up."

Experienced team members are wise to the trap. They figure it is better to hold back and abstain because it is all going to change sooner rather than later.

Creating a Culture of Success is not an initiative or a program.

CULTURE IS

- For-real
- Forever
- Your organization's DNA
- Who you are

> Culture takes sustained effort from the beginning and throughout the life of your organization. Particularly in the early days and weeks, the messages about the new culture must be constantly repeated and reinforced. If you don't, it will be gone and forgotten within 90 days.

MAKE IT VISIBLE

Display your finalized Culture Guide prominently in places where it will be seen by one and all every working day. Post it permanently in the break room and set it apart from other postings by laminating it. Better yet, frame it and make it attractive enough to display another framed copy where people work. Distribute copies to everyone in the organization. You can laminate these, too, to reinforce the idea of importance and permanence.

Years ago, a business owner we work with began spotlighting culture in a very artistic way. He had a local muralist paint significant events that shaped the culture of his organization in the form of a border around the top of the office break room walls. Periodically, the muralist returns to add new images, words and phrases to emphasize cultural points. After a recent meeting where we focused on key concepts of a Culture of Success, the muralist went to work to codify the cultural concepts on the walls of the lunchroom. The message is clear: What goes on the wall is important to us. It's an effective graphical reminder for the team, and a nice, classy decorative element in the room where everybody comes frequently during the course of a day.

The message has high impact in that particular room, because team members see it during downtime, exactly when they might otherwise be prone to complaining, backbiting, making fun of others behind their backs, and other nastiness that passes for fun in Culture by Default workplaces. The mural makes countercultural behavior less welcome.

MAKE IT LEGENDARY

Keep your Culture of Success principles fresh and compelling by telling stories that illustrate them in action and make emotional connections. Until there's some history and the team has had time to develop its own lore and cultural heroes, tap into your own life and feelings.

One story I tell my team involves a boyhood experience of a key Culture Guide expectation – Follow Up.

At age 8 I rode the city bus to and from swimming lessons. One day a driver-in-training closed the door on me, so I was caught with my leg sticking out of the bus as she pulled away from the stop. The driver, a supervisor training her, and passengers could not have been more concerned and solicitous, but I was fine. Once at home something extraordinary happened. A high executive of our municipal transportation authority called to ask if I was okay. Cynics will think he called to ward off a lawsuit, but people were not so litigious back then. He, as chief representative of his team, simply felt that he had a responsibility to follow up and leave no loose ends, and thus made an indelible impression on my mind. That's what I think about when I think of Follow Up.

After I tell the story, it's also what my team thinks about. An abstract concept comes alive with a story behind it, images, and emotion. People know why this principle of our culture especially matters to me.

Making shared truths legendary, to be remembered and retold, is as old as humankind's ability to communicate in words. The Bible and other religious books are not theology texts but books of stories that illustrate spiritual truths. Legends impart business wisdom, too, both within organizations and to the world at large.

One management classic involves Sam Walton, founder of Walmart and leader of a revolution in retailing. He made surprise drop-ins on company operations, including legendary, unannounced visits to Walmart distribution centers at 4 a.m. where he climbed into truck cabs and rode along on deliveries to stores.

Walton's time was worth many thousands of dollars an hour, but this was time well spent for him and the company because it kept him connected with people in the trenches. And it had an impact on all of his company's hundreds of thousands of employees. The story of Walton's actions sent a message – "We're all in this together" – far more effectively than the words alone. The story showed, too, that in Walton's organization no one was too good for any job that needed doing. The lesson lives on within Walmart. It lives on outside the company, too – I just retold it, didn't I? It's especially significant here because Walton's predawn drop-ins and truck rides really were all about company culture.

As time goes on, create your own book of legends, with short, memorable stories that illustrate how to live your Culture of Success.

MAKE IT OFTEN

Review one aspect of your Culture Guide at daily meetings. It takes just a moment to read aloud an expectation like "Keep it Fun" or "Early is On Time" and remind people to live it today. Emails reinforce such messages, too. As I often stress, words are not actions, but they plant the ideas that lead to actions and help keep people from backsliding into old bad habits. If you don't continually exert a positive influence, somebody else is going to fill your silence with the wrong kind of messages and load up the bandwidth with negativity.

Reiterating messages about the new culture is education in the truest sense. The only purpose of education, in my book, is **results producing action**. Knowledge with no action is pointless. Messages that get repeated frequently are remembered, get acted upon and get results.

MAKE IT HABITUAL

Never forget:

> It takes 7 to 12 repetitions to fix something new in the mind.
>
> You have to know it before you can do it.
>
> It takes 21 days to make it a habit.

But the habit won't last without reinforcement.

Make it your habit to keep your Culture of Success fresh in the team's mind. Get the message out about every point in the Culture Guide, and keep repeating it. Make culture part of the everyday conversation. Make it come alive all the time – first, last and most often.

Think, Do –

❑ Plan a rollout that will make a positive, lasting impression.

❑ Put culture prominently on display. Print it. Laminate it. Frame it. Hand it out. Have it painted on the walls.

❑ Identify stories from your own or the team's past that you can tell to illustrate why each aspect of your Culture Guide is important.

❑ Schedule reminders and discussions of each Culture Guide point and fresh ways to put them on display.

THE LAW OF RECOGNITION

NATURAL LAW:
We repeat what gains us recognition.

THE ENDURING POWER OF 'I APPRECIATE'

Just last weekend I worked with an office team that included a woman I helped to train 18 years ago. In the session I brought up a very simple but effective way to show appreciation and gratitude to a teammate that we've taught for years, the *I Appreciate Note*. We make writing such notes an absolute no-brainer by giving out pads of pages with blanks to fill in:

I appreciate _____ *because* _____.
Thanks for making it happen, _____.

So simple, and yet so significant. The woman from years back said she still had every one of the *I Appreciates* teammates gave her when they first got their pads 18 years ago. The messages had meaning she treasured.

The story shows how precious just a little bit of recognition from others can be. This is true for two main reasons: 1) This is a fundamental psychological need. 2) People are absolutely starved for it, particularly in workplace settings.

In regards to reason two, I am continually amazed how rarely management makes even minimal efforts to recognize team members for their efforts. Speaking a few approving words takes no time and costs nothing, but leaders don't make the effort. This is to the detriment of themselves and their businesses, because people work, first and foremost, to be recognized for their efforts. We crave significance and need to know that we matter and make a difference for others – which we can't know until others give us **recognition**.

After recognition, the number-two motivator in the workplace is **challenge**. People want to feel like winners.

Personal growth through work is number three.

Money comes in fourth. If this surprises you, you have a lot of company.

Money rises in importance only when it's in critically short supply. But when financial compensation is reasonable, it stays low on the list. The psychologist Frederick Herzberg, who did pioneering studies of motivation in the workplace, assigned money to a lower order of factors in job satisfaction which cause dissatisfaction in their absence but can't satisfy in themselves. Herzberg showed that gratification and happiness result from psychological and social factors such as feelings of competency and status. His findings were in line with the theories of a fellow pioneer in motivational psychology, Abraham Maslow, who developed the famous *Maslow's Hierarchy of Needs*. Maslow put needs in a category he called Esteem, including respect from others, on the next-to-highest level. Both Herzberg and Maslow used different terms for it, but they both taught that recognition by others is a prime need and motivator in the workplace.

This is especially true in regards to culture. Perpetuating a Culture of Success requires the person in charge to encourage behavior congruent with the culture through recognition in front of the team and in private. On the flip side, it also requires that incongruent behavior be recognized, confronted, and stopped.

WHAT IS THE OPPOSITE OF LOVE?

This might seem like one of those rhetorical questions, good for thoughtful discussion but not much else. But it bears directly on the subject.

And the answer isn't hate, as many people we ask immediately answer. Love and hate can be very closely related, driven by similar – or the same – intense personal feelings. Spurned lovers hate with a passion, then reconcile and flip back to passionate love. If you hate somebody or something, you care a lot. The object of hate *matters*.

The opposite of love – indifference – means you don't care at all. Indifference to others says they're nothing, devoid of significance. In the workplace, indifference is very destructive to people and their job performance.

An oft-cited experiment by Herzberg showed how employees respond to anything that even looks like attentiveness on the part of management. The experiment was designed to test the relationship of lighting on the productivity of factory workers. Not surprisingly, output went up with brighter lighting. But then it also improved when lights were lowered. It turned out that any change, bright or dim, had a positive effect. Why? Because higher-ups bothered to make changes. This was the lowest, rock-bottom form of recognition – that there were human beings down on the factory floor that management wasn't entirely indifferent to – and workers responded to it.

WATCH WHAT YOU RECOGNIZE

Because you'll get it.

And beware the Law of Unintended Consequences. You may unknowingly reward behavior that undermines your culture.

Say, for instance, your ideal culture encourages thorough, solid preparation, detail-mindedness, and performance on time and by the numbers – but you heap praise on those who save the day during crisis situations. Now and again, this is great, because crises arise and days do need saving. But if that's what you single out for recognition more than the quiet, solid diligence and competence that you really want – which prevents crises! – you're sending the wrong messages.

For one, the hero of the hour is not going about his or her duties in ways congruent with the culture, while those who do so earn no praise. And there's danger that crises will be allowed to happen, because they bring praise and glory.

Recognition is the outward manifestation of your own inward values. So you need to look deep and think about what you really want from your people, then make sure you recognize actions consistent with the Culture of Success you are building. If you recognize somebody's hard work, you'll get more hard work from everybody. If you recognize results, people will focus on results. And what you don't recognize, you won't get.

RECOGNITION 101: LATE GUY BECOMES EARLY BIRD

Every office has somebody who habitually shows up after starting time. People make a joke of it, but the late arrival is a disruption and a burden on others. Your late guy was Charlie. When the "Be early" item in the Culture Guide came up in a team meeting, Charlie said this: "You know, showing up to work on time is my biggest struggle. But I've got five alarm clocks now, I set them earlier and put them all over the house, and I will get here early!"

Lo and behold, Charlie lives up to his words. Early on you give him a quiet attaboy so he knows you notice.

Later at a team meeting you say this: "You'll all remember that Charlie made a commitment, and for the past three weeks he's been here early every morning. I just want to thank him for making the effort to make the change, which helps all of us."

Charlie will remain an early bird, because recognition just made his extra effort worthwhile.

It's so quick, easy, simple, but it's astounding how rarely words like these are spoken.

In the press of what seems like more important, substantive business under discussion, it's easy to let recognition slide. But if you do, you're abrogating an important responsibility of leadership. Make recognition an unwritten item on your meeting agendas. Recognize people's efforts one-on-one, too.

> All it takes is a moment to single somebody out, acknowledge him or her, and say "thanks."
>
> Consider it part of your job.

AWARD CEREMONY

"Be a willing WIT," is a catch phrase we teach and make a basic principle of our own team culture. The WIT stands for "Whatever it takes," which is what team members do when something really needs doing. They do it regardless of title and job description, because it's everybody's responsibility to go above and beyond and pitch in. "That's not my job," is absolutely unacceptable around here and in all Willing WIT cultures.

One company we work with established a Willing WIT Award, presented once a month at team meetings. Each winner chooses the following month's recipient and presents the award, explaining how the new winner earned this recognition. Making the award reciprocal, up and down the job hierarchy, reinforces the idea that everybody matters and has a stake in the Culture of Success. It also encourages team members to recognize each other's efforts. Earning respect from peers for a job well done is at least as important as recognition by leadership.

If there's a cultural value you especially want to focus on and strengthen, create an award for it.

'I APPRECIATE' NOTES

They work. Be sure to let people know it's okay to appreciate the leaders, too, if they earn it.

BE SINCERE

Recognizing others' efforts and saying nice things may, at first, take people way out of their comfort zones. This is a sad commentary on the prevailing culture of the entire working world, where peer-to-peer chatter tends to be nasty, and talk about the organization focuses on the negative. It doesn't need to be this way, but it is until somebody expends the effort to make things more positive.

In negative cultures, giving an *I appreciate* to the boss, as I just suggested, is unthinkable because it may appear to be solicitous and manipulative. Admittedly, it could be just that – but only if you are insincere.

On the other hand, good words that you truly mean are almost always welcome. Leaders are people too, and they need recognition, acknowledgement, and encouragement just like everybody else.

Manipulators try to use insincere praise and flattery to their own advantage, but people are not so easy to fool (unless they want to be). We human beings are pretty good at smoking out manipulation. Insincerity for supposedly good purposes doesn't fly either. Don't give strokes just because you think somebody needs attention and cheering up.

Recognition should be earned and sincerely meant.

LOUD SILENCE

Failure to recognize individual and group efforts to live your Culture of Success looks and feels like indifference. It sends the message that this is not important. It erodes and will eventually destroy the culture. Never forget that your people watch your every move and listen to every word. And what you *don't* say and do speaks volumes.

RECOGNITION BY DEFAULT

Fail to recognize and confront behavior that is not in keeping with the culture and you have effectively crossed out a rule in the Culture Guide.

Passivity is one of the many paths of least resistance you absolutely do not want to follow. It sends a clear message that the bad behavior in question is really acceptable. It doesn't take much of this for the team to get the idea – from the example you set – that all the rules are bendable and that you don't necessarily mean what you say.

Some leaders kid themselves that they're being friendly by letting a misbehaver off the hook, as if winking and saying "Aw, I don't want to make a big deal out of this," is a way to bond and be a good guy. But you're not being a good person or a friend. Permissiveness is really a form of indifference, and it destroys relationships instead of building them. Insisting that someone live up to team expectations shows much more care and respect. In this regard we're still like children, wanting to know there are boundaries and exactly where they are.

CONFRONTING INCONGRUENT BEHAVIOR – THE EYE-ROLLER

This sort of thing happens all the time, and it's easy to let slide because it's mostly about attitude and facial expression:

At a team meeting, for the umpteenth time, Joanne rolls her eyes, sighs, and makes snarky comments under her breath whenever Ben has something to say.

It is time to put a stop to this. Here's how:

Either call a break or wait for the next one if it's coming up shortly. Pull Joanne aside for a private conversation.

In a calm, value-neutral way, give a factual account of what you just witnessed – her eye-rolling, sighing, comments, etc. And say something like this: "This concerns me because it's not respectful of your team member, and not in keeping with the culture everybody – including you – agreed to live by."

This gets you to an important *Ask*: "Will you be willing, when we go back into the meeting, to apologize to everybody, so they know you know you acted against our team culture?"

Joanne has no good answer but "Yes" – and she'll be a better, more respected team member after she makes her apology.

It's tempting to put on a show of old-time disapproval and judgement: "That was the rudest, most disrespectful…!" Don't, because it's far more effective to keep things factual and tied to culture and have the errant employee take corrective measures.

BE CONGRUENT

This is a challenge, because it's so easy to fall back on old habits.

Let's say somebody comes into your office complaining about another team member – she's late, messy, doesn't do her work, and so on. Rather than listening, or yelling at the complainer to pay attention to his own job and not bother you with such nonsense, you need to stop the complaining cold and create a moment of recognition that this is incongruent with the culture.

Just say: "I appreciate your concern. You'll remember that we all agreed to take problems back to the source. Have you talked to her about this?"

If the answer is "no," as it probably is, say this: "I have every confidence that if you do that, you two can work it out. If you can't, come back together and we'll talk, the three of us."

If somebody comes in with a more technical, job-specific problem, act in accordance with another key Culture Guide expectation – Be Solution-Minded. Our version says that when you identify a problem, you also identify at least three solutions, one of which doesn't cost anything.

Your appropriate response is, "What do you suggest be done about it?"

The stock, non-cultural answer is, "I don't know. But I thought you'd want to know there's a problem."

You should come back like this: "I do appreciate your bringing this to my attention. Since you are so close to the situation, would you be willing to give it some thought and come back with some possible solutions?"

Again, you've reinforced the culture.

This isn't as head-on and obvious as singling people out for praise or confronting overt misbehavior, but it's still all about recognition. You're recognizing the team member and what he or she is trying to do vis-à-vis culture, and showing how to live the culture. By so doing, you're living it, too.

PEER-TO-PEER CULTURE

Another tough one, because people are reluctant to correct colleagues and work friends for fear of coming off holier-than-thou or bossy. But if a Culture of Success is going to thrive, your people have to feel free to actively support it and stop incongruent behavior. This is something that needs to be talked-about and actively encouraged. And people should know they don't need to be jerks to help keep others on-track.

There is, for instance, a friendly and perfectly respectful way to shut down insulting talk behind each other's backs, a conversational staple and a plague of negativity and bad feelings in workplaces.

Let's say Team Member A plops down by Team Member B and starts trash-talking C. B should stop A and ask if whatever's wrong with C upsets A and, if so, has A talked to C about it? After the probable answer to the second question – "No" – B can offer to take A to C, if it's uncomfortable to go over alone.

Most likely A will back off, because the trash talk is more about vindictive entertainment than a problem that needs to be addressed. But whatever the outcome, the behind-the-back talk stopped. At the very least, A won't start up with B again.

This takes some courage on B's part, but it also sends an important message that B can be trusted to shoot straight and not talk about A behind A's back, or other people behind their backs.

A link in the chain of negativity has been broken. If it keeps up, your workplace will be revolutionized.

WIRING IN POSITIVITY

My company is actually a team of teams that work in different offices. We have a daily exercise where each team reports in with the *best* things that happened that day. This provides a chance for teams to recognize each other's wins and their own. It also prevents griping about what went wrong, which can dominate office chatter unless you turn it around.

One office had a Murphy's Law day, one disaster after another, some of which the team endured in unbearable Texas heat because the air conditioning compressor went out. The best things reported by that team were that the AC didn't fail until afternoon, and tomorrow will surely be better. Nobody griped. Nobody else said "Poor you." Instead, the folks who had the snake-bit day earned recognition for their spirit and sense of humor. They gave themselves recognition, too. They were Culture of Success heroes.

Think, Do –

❏ Form the habit of informally recognizing someone for something they did at least once a day.

❏ Watch for improvement and recognize it.

❏ Formalize recognition and make it part of every team meeting with awards and acknowledging efforts to live your Culture of Success.

❏ Institute and implement the organization-wide use of *I Appreciate Notes*.

❏ Practice your verbal skills by rehearsing ways to tactfully confront and stop culturally incongruent behavior.

THE LAW OF ATTRACTION

NATURAL LAW:

You attract – and are attracted to – others just like you.

Vernacular Version: Birds of a feather flock together. So be careful who you're flockin' with!

IT AIN'T THE TEAM

Lately I had a talk with a client who had reached a point where she could take her company to a new level. With a little more help from my team she could boost output and revenue and grow her business dramatically. She had everything to gain, and she knew it, but turned down the opportunity.

"I don't think I'm ready," she said, "because I don't have the right team."

In her judgment, her people would not step up to a new challenge. They were unwilling, incapable, or both.

I hear this sort of thing more than you'd imagine and always have similar thoughts – "Whoa, who hired those people? And who let them slide into the sorry state they're in, where you assume they're not going to perform?"

In due time I usually say it, in more diplomatic terms, and tell them, "If you don't have the right team, maybe your team doesn't have the right leader. Maybe you need to work on yourself...."

In truth, there isn't a lot of "maybe" about it. Any time somebody says, "I don't have the right team," alarm bells ring, because there are problems at the top.

MORE ALARMS

They go off for me when leaders get to the same point as the woman above, face-to-face with a new opportunity that is theirs if they want it, and say something like, "That sounds just great, but let me go back and run it by my people, see what they think..."

This is a leader trying to fob off responsibility for making important decisions on others. He or she may also perceive leadership as a popularity contest and feel the need for personal affirmation and support.

What I want to hear is this: "Great, Steve. I'm going to tell the team this is something under consideration and ask for input. I'll get back to you with my decision."

Note whose decision it is. Back home the boss gives the same message to the team: "I would love your opinions, which I'll consider before I make up my mind and let you know. Whether or not you like my decision, I expect you to get on board." That's culture-congruent leadership talking.

IN YOUR IMAGE

Look in your mirror. Look at your team. You're looking at the same thing – a reflection of *you*. Leaders tend to hire in their own image and create teams that fit their own idiosyncrasies. Something about the people on your team attracted you, or they wouldn't be with you. And something about you attracted your people. If you're seeing things you don't like, the first place to look for solutions is within. Look deep and figure out what's going on and what needs changing.

Birds of a feather: The good news is, we human birds can decide to grow new feathers and transform from barnyard fowl to soaring rulers of the sky. The leader helps the whole flock to fly higher.

REMEMBER THE ALAMO

Organizations change. They evolve, as do the individuals in them. They have to, because ever-changing reality gives us a simple, stark choice:

Adapt or die.

Every once in a while things come to a head – as they do when you and your workplace team commit to winning a cultural revolution – and it's time to have what I call a Colonel William Travis Moment.

A little historic background: In the mid-1830s, Texans fought for independence from Mexico. Travis led 200 or so men in a heroic last stand against a huge Mexican army in an old mission in San Antonio called the Alamo. All the Texans died fighting, which gave their side a battle cry – Remember the Alamo! – and turned the tide of the war. On the eve of the final, fateful battle, Travis drew a line on the ground with his sword and asked those who wanted to stand and fight to cross the line with him. Only one man stayed on the "Thanks but no thanks" side of the line and fled during the night. The rest crossed and became heroes who are revered to this day.

The stakes for you are not life and death, thank heaven, but the principles of leadership are the same. To redefine workplace culture, you must do what Travis did – draw a line between what was and what will be and ask your team to cross the line with you, embrace the new way of behaving and getting along with each other, and live up to new, higher expectations.

When you draw the line, acknowledge that this may not be everybody's cup of tea, but that's okay. Those who don't want to get on-board should come to you, and you'll do everything you can to help them find other organizations that fit.

But don't be surprised if the whole bunch comes over to the Culture of Success side of the line and lives up to expectations. You may be underestimating your people, as I'm sure the woman in charge who passed up a golden opportunity was. You have heroes in your midst who will – if you draw a line and challenge them to cross it – amaze you. They'll amaze themselves, too.

HOPE FOR BAD EGGS

Even your worst backbiter trash talker sower-of-negativity Bad Egg (BE) can come around. I've seen it happen.

One of three things occurs when a BE encounters a new Culture of Success:

- The BE fights change tooth and nail, refusing to get on-board and thereby challenging your leadership and sabotaging what you and team members intend to accomplish.

- The BE gets with the program and becomes a better egg, because there's no choice and maybe the BE wasn't so bad to begin with.

- The BE can't pull off 1 because you won't allow it to happen, and discomfort compels him/her to leave the team.

Though 2 happens quite often, there are hardcore incorrigibles who will, if you let them, exert negative leadership. But that occurs only when the leader fails to fulfill the duty to lead, with a 100 percent commitment to building and maintaining the culture.

As for 3, sometimes even not-so-bad eggs feel uncomfortable on your team. No matter how much everybody else is in-sync and loving it, not every workplace is for everybody, and that's okay. It doesn't happen often, but I'm actually happy when a team member comes to me and says the culture just isn't a good fit. I consider this very healthy and do my best to help that person find a suitable job somewhere else.

DREAM TEAM RECRUITMENT

> Never forget: One person can significantly alter the
> prevailing workplace culture – for good or for bad.

It is, therefore, critically important to make smart, culturally
congruent hires. How they go about their work truly is more
important than how good they are when they first hire on. You
can teach the how-to, but you can't do nearly as much about
such personal attributes as disposition, spirit, ability and desire
to get along with others. Zero in on your ideal new hire by
using your Culture Guide through the entire hiring process.

FIRST, RE-READ THE GUIDE YOURSELF

And live up to it during interviewing and hiring.

Start at the appointed time. This, of course, means being at
your desk early. Some bosses routinely make people wait
to project power and send the message that their time is
worth more than everybody else's. But lateness really sends a
message that punctuality isn't a big deal for you and that you
consider yourself special.

Be ready. The first impression should be that you're expecting
the candidate and are thoroughly prepared, with paperwork in
front of you and command of the relevant facts because you
did your research. A harried, disorganized boss doesn't look
busy, just harried and disorganized.

Be warm. Probably one of your cultural expectations is to show caring for teammates. Do so with this prospective teammate, too. Appreciate the effort it took to get there to give you a chance to meet and review the candidate's qualifications. Don't overdo the warm-fuzzy, but you want a conversation that's not just another cold, static interview.

The Law of Example operates here, because you do more than say what's important – you show it. The Law of Primacy comes into play, too, because the first contact with you, the head of the team, makes the most vivid and lasting impression. Should you hire the candidate, you want to plant the image of culture congruence at the leadership level, because that's what will be remembered.

THE CANDIDATE AND THE GUIDE

After initial interviewing, introduce the candidates that interested you to the Culture Guide. Provide time for them to read it, making sure the points are understood.

Say, "If we choose to offer you a position, these are the things we expect you to live up to." Speak the words with clarity and seriousness to emphasize that following the Guide is as much a part of the job as productive tasks. On your team, culture is not an option.

Then you can zoom out and explain the point of creating and maintaining a great workplace culture. In interviews I like to tell people that I have yet to meet anybody who didn't want to work in a terrific, positive environment where people feel their best and do their best. Nor have I met anybody who said, "You know, I don't care how others treat me. Just pay me and abuse me however you want." This is good for a smile, but also true.

SEEING THEM SEEING THE LIGHT

Be sure your candidate gets it, because this is all new. Chances are he or she has never had experience with a business that put such a high priority on workplace culture and emphasized behaving well and treating each other decently while on the job.

The right kind of people catch on pretty quickly, then light up and exude enthusiasm – "Wow, this is great!" "I wish the other places I worked had this." "This sounds just amazing."

Of course everybody tries to figure out what you want to hear and give it you. But real enthusiasm is hard to fake. Watch body language and facial expression and you'll know when a job candidate is truly ready to embrace your Culture of Success.

DISQUALIFIERS

If the person reads through the Culture Guide, says something to the effect of, "Okay, I get it," in a perfunctory sort of way, and moves on, you're looking at signs of trouble. Either the message about the importance of culture didn't sink in, or you're seeing surface indications of doubt, with inner voices saying things like, "Ooh, this is tough. I have to show up early, be nice to people, do work that's not in my job description. It's not worth it..."

Next.

Pay close attention to what people say about previous jobs and the people they worked with. Negative judgments and harsh words are red flags. If they talk negatively and throw their old bosses under the bus, guess who's going to be next? You and your management team, that's who. Other staffers will get bad-mouthed too, guaranteed.

In my own hiring model, anybody who shows up late for a job interview is immediately disqualified. I'm always amazed when it happens, but it does. Short of a car accident or serious medical problem, there's no excuse – especially not "I'm sorry, I got lost." A candidate who truly cared about making the right impression would do what my consulting teams do when they go to a new and unfamiliar location. The night before they're scheduled to begin, they map out and follow the route from their hotel to the destination, build in extra time and show up – per our Culture Guide – early.

And they're not even applying for the job, because they've already got it!

BE REAL

There are four possible decisions here – yours to offer a job or not; and the candidate's to accept or not – which will, ultimately, be made in accordance with the natural law spotlighted in the introductory chapter, The Law of Emotion, which states that people primarily make decisions emotionally, then justify their decisions with logic.

In the end you'll be swayed by your feelings, and so will your job candidate, and afterward you'll both rationalize your "Yes" or "No" with facts and reasoning that may be very sound. But first you'll do what feels right.

Note that "emotional" and "irrational" are not one in the same. You can educate your emotions and give yourself and your candidate opportunities to deepen feelings about things that really matter, which is what screening and hiring with the Culture Guide is all about. The more exposure to reality, the better.

When you have a prime candidate and are close to making a decision, you can administer a day long dose of reality with a Work Assessment Day. A paid tryout in the workplace environment, interacting with team members, reveals so much about a person's culture fit. You want him or her to be comfortable, but you also want to watch every move that relates to communicating and getting along. Just as important, the candidate has a chance to make a better personal judgment about whether your workplace is right.

> **WARNING**: There's another natural law at work here, which is not covered in this book. It says, basically, that people like to be liked. The law is one of those truths that can seem so obvious that people overlook it, but it can cloud judgment and cause people to do things just to be liked by other people. This is especially true where people assess each other and make yes or no decisions. Everybody tries to put the best foot forward in order to wow the other person and make the sale.

Be wowed too easily, you may find yourself with a new employee who settles in, gets comfortable, and starts taking liberties, who is nothing like the person you thought you hired. By the same token, you want to resist the urge to dazzle a prime job candidate and be truthful about what signing on to a Culture of Success means. It calls for a commitment and sustained effort that's above and beyond the norm. It's not for everybody.

THE WAY TO GET MARRIED

I compare the screening and hiring process to my courtship of Cheryl, who has been my wife for over 20 years which get ever more wonderful. Once I realized that our relationship was going somewhere, I dropped the usual dating game and told her that from then on, I was going to be totally transparent and brutally honest about myself and my expectations. I told her why, too. Everybody gets excited on the front end, but then the years go by and they discover things they dearly wish they knew back at the beginning. I told Cheryl that 5-10-20 years in the future, I wanted her to be able to look me in the eye and say this was better than she thought it would be.

So far, so good.

> For team members, my goal is to provide a job that gets better than they ever thought it could be, and keeps getting better.

Do I always hit the mark? Of course not. Judgments about other human beings can be off. But the mark gets hit a lot more because there is a goal, and a system for attaining it – hiring with the Culture Guide.

THE FIRST SIX MONTHS

They're going to be less stressful and more productive for your new team members because culture-conscious hiring eliminates so much uncertainty. Normally people spend the first six months tiptoeing around and behaving with exaggerated care, trying to learn all the unwritten rules and finding out where the mines are buried and where they can feel safe. The Culture of Success declares the whole place to be a zone of safety for one and all.

It isn't just the new team member who benefits – it's everybody, including the leader. Since he or she knew up front what expectations are, he or she is far more likely to meet them, thereby saving a lot of frustration on the part of fellow team members and the leader. Fast-forwarding initial adjustment puts the focus on productive work. Again, the Culture of Success goes straight to the bottom line.

From the very first contact with a prospective team member, it pays off to raise the flag of your Culture of Success and your Guide, which is the team's cultural *Pledge of Allegiance*. The ideal isn't always daily reality, but it's something everybody strives to live up to.

Think, Do –

❏ Know this, and don't forget it: If you expect to hire culturally congruent people, you must live the culture – especially during the hiring process.

❏ Always introduce the Culture Guide and discuss it before you make a formal offer.

❏ Watch body language and listen carefully to gauge candidates' enthusiasm and cultural compatibility.

❏ If possible, give them an opportunity to show how well they fit with a Work Assessment Day.

❏ Pay close attention to your own feelings and intuition about whether a given job candidate will be a good team member.

THE LAW OF ATTRIBUTES

NATURAL LAW:

People take on the most powerful attributes of their surroundings – the physical environment and the people around them.

You are a product of your environment. So choose the environment that will best develop you toward your objective. Analyze your life in terms of its environment. Are the things around you helping you toward success – or are they holding you back?

– W. Clement Stone

A TALE OF TWO TABLES

A furniture swap became part of the deal when we sold our old house before moving into the house my family now calls home. The buyers really liked our dining room table, which fit its room perfectly. They also happened to have a nice table that would comfortably seat the two parents and six children (there's now a seventh) in our family, which would go well in our new house. So when the buyers offered to trade tables, it made good sense to say yes.

I didn't give this much thought until the family sat down to eat, and I noticed a profound alteration in our family's mealtime culture. Suddenly the kids spoke up on their own, with no need to draw them out. Even the normally quiet ones jumped in and talked freely. The younger members of the family held up their end of conversations with the teenagers and grown-ups. Give-and-take was livelier, and conversations lasted longer, to the point that we sometimes lingered at the table after we ate just to keep talking. The whole social dynamic of mealtime changed.

Why? Because our new table was round.

At our old table, which was rectangular, things had been more formal and restrained. The shape put Dad at the head of the table and implied a traditional paternal hierarchy. Roundness set us free of all that, with an arrangement that says everybody has an equal voice.

After the dinner table revelation, I began to encourage clients to change the shape of the tables where they meet to work and brainstorm together. Round tables have the same effects in the workplace as in my dining room and help make the Culture of Success come to life.

I guess I shouldn't have been surprised by the significance of circular seating. After all, table shape is celebrated in one of the oldest legends in the English language, the story of King Arthur and the Knights of the Round Table. A table with square corners wouldn't have been worth mentioning, much less sharing the billing with Arthur's knights. But in the brutally hierarchical medieval culture, Arthur's table was revolutionary, implying that others could engage in give-and-take with the king.

CREATED BY OUR CREATIONS

> "We shape our buildings, and afterwards our buildings shape us."

The immortal British leader and orator Winston Churchill spoke this wisdom about the relationship of people and the spaces they work and live in. At first a human-made environment reflects its makers. But then people take on the attributes of their surroundings. A workplace environment can either reinforce or detract from a Culture of Success.

Churchill's words were spoken about the Houses of Parliament, which I visited while I was in London to give a speech, where I had a very moving experience of the power of a structure to bring out the best in people. German bombing during World War II destroyed the chamber of the House of Commons. The rebuilt chamber looks like it did before the war except for one bomb-scarred section of the entryway that Churchill ordered to remain as it was. In that same entryway stands a statue of Churchill himself, now cordoned off because so many members of the House of Commons touched Churchill's shoe for good luck. They hoped some of the great man's oratorical genius would wear off on them.

The chamber's architecture speaks of the long history and tradition of the rule of law in England, and also the need to protect it from enemies. The damaged entryway stands as a constant reminder that freedom is fragile and that decisions made in this place will ultimately determine the country's future. In the decades since World War II, the message continues to resound. It always will.

> What you choose to place in your environment influences organizational culture.

MEETING OF MINDS

My team and I live by and teach the Master Mind Principle, which was developed by the pioneer of modern motivational philosophy Napoleon Hill. The principle states that two or more people who work in harmony for a shared purpose tap into a creative intelligence far greater than their own – the Master Mind – which combines the brainpower and talents of everyone involved.

My team and I, who encourage everybody to form Master Mind groups, have a sort of Master Master Mind made up of high-level clients. Once a year we hold a meeting for this group that pulls in more than 1,000 people.

Early on, we went with the typical default setup for large-audience presentations at convention hotels, with chairs in long, straight lines facing a raised speaker's platform at one end of the room. But I saw that the geometry worked directly against the culture we wanted to reinforce. It sent messages that were all about command and control – sit down, pay attention to the person at the podium and nobody else. The experience was more solo than shared, because when you sat in the crowd and looked forward, all you saw of fellow audience members were their backs.

It took a little persuading to get hotel staffers to break pattern, but we rearranged our meetings so chairs were in rows that curved around the platform for a theater in the half-round effect. People still faced the speaker, but also hundreds of others, whose expressions they could see and react to. Just that visual contact created an interactive experience. Our setup now said that what happens on stage is still important, but we're all in this together and want to share the experience. The impact of the change was amazing. It transformed the whole dynamic of the meeting.

> For groups of any size, organized for any purpose, your setting and your setup either reinforces or detracts from your chosen culture.

STAND UP, DRESS UP

Seating, or lack thereof, plays a role in a highly effective tactic to reinforce culture at a smaller-scale daily event: the morning work team meeting. Have your people meet while standing. Sitting makes it possible to go limp and zone out, which is hard to do on your feet. Standing also keeps meetings short and focused and encourages people to get the day off to a good start – wide-awake, upbeat, eager for action.

Proper dress has a similar effect that lasts all day.

Clothes really are a wearable environment. A friend of mine tells a story about the hazards of letting people come to work looking like slobs. He tried one, and only one, Casual Friday. It was a catastrophe that saw performance go straight down the tubes. This might seem surprising, because nobody outside the company ever sees my friend's team members do their jobs. He owns a large call center where, theoretically, staffers could work in Halloween costumes or pajamas and people on the other end of the line would be no wiser. But dressing down dragged them down.

On the subject of dress, I am adamantly against team members in the health care professions wearing scrubs, which in my book are worse than Friday business casual. People who wear scrubs tend to treat them like pajamas, which is pretty much what they are, and make the wrong impression on the wearer, teammates, and patients. Unless they're a necessity, as in operating rooms, lose the scrubs and dress in business attire. It makes a huge difference when male medical professionals wear neckties. A dress shirt and a narrow strip of cloth change the environment and the whole experience of being part of the practice.

> Dressing up says the work you do is worth dressing up for. It's a reminder that your job is a performance in front of others whom you don't want to let down.

SHOW TIME

Think about recording and broadcast facilities, which have light-up signs outside their inner sanctums, the studios, that read "On Air." Seeing those words lit adds urgency and a note of caution – big things are now in progress, so be very careful of what you do. You get the same effect backstage at a live performance.

You can give your team the same pre-performance energy with a simple sign – "You're On stage" – at the employee entrance or the inside of the break room door, where they'll see it coming out. This message is literally true. Your workplace is a performance space. You set the stage so it supports your cultural values and the story you want to tell. You dress for your role and play it, so others see the best of who you are as individuals and as a team.

THESE WALLS REALLY CAN TALK

And they do talk to anybody who comes into your space. In a business of any kind, the things that are there by design, or by accident, tell more about you and your people than you imagine.

A study by researcher Sam Gosling at the University of Texas, later popularized by Malcolm Gladwell in his book on high-speed thought processes *Blink*, showed how much people can tell about others from spending just 15 minutes in their offices or living spaces when they're not present. Assessments of personality traits by total strangers, based only on looking at personal space, turned out to be as good or better than those of longtime friends of the people those spaces belonged to. In business, the implication is that your customers can come in, look around, and see important attributes of you and your team reflected in physical surroundings. Experiencing the human environment tells them much more. Most importantly, it tells them if this is a place where they want to be. Your environment projects to others your internal culture.

REVOLUTION BY DESIGN

One of our clients, who happens to be a dentist, radically rearranged both team culture and his office environment in ways both team members and patients love, which totally upends the way dental practices traditionally look and operate.

Sad to say, the normal medical office experience is a lot like a post office where patients are packages, to be shunted from front desk to treatment room to the payment window and appointments clerk – at each point being punched, stamped, postmarked, and processed. Our bold practitioner got rid of the front desk, so the patient spends the first moments in a lovely living room that would do a fine home proud, where a team member appears, bids the patient welcome and conducts him or her to the treatment room chair, which in a modern dental office offers spa-level comfort.

For the rest of the visit, the patient stays right in the chair, as team members come to take care of paperwork, financial arrangements, scheduling appointments, and all the other incidentals around the main event – professional attention and treatment. At the conclusion of the appointment, the patient is accompanied to the front door by a team member, with no further tasks to be completed.

This is an amazing experience for patients and the team, who learn every aspect of running the practice and combine efforts to take care of patients. For the system to work, everybody has to be cross-trained for tasks that aren't normally part of their jobs. There are still specialists in such areas as finance, insurance, and scheduling, but people need to know much more than usual about what teammates do, because they actually do it. Teammates truly have each other's backs, and the system promotes understanding, empathy, and mutual respect because people understand the complexities and challenges of what others do.

In this case, the physical environment and the human environment are inextricably linked. Such a unique culture has to have a unique home, and vice versa.

360-DEGREE CULTURE

The physical environment, with all the things you place in it by careful design, is like a shell that gives shape to what goes on inside – the human environment where your team works and interacts, which shapes them. As soon as they walk through the door, people start to sync up with others in mind and, to a surprising extent, in body. Scientific studies have shown that vital signs change and trend toward the average for people in the same space. Meanwhile, the interpersonal matrix they tie into is almost unimaginably complex. Do the math and you'll see why. In a team of two, there are two relationship pathways: A to B and B to A. Introduce a third team member, you multiply relationship pathways exponentially: A to B, B to A, A to B and C together, B and C back to A, and so on, for nine interpersonal pathways. Adding a team member is never simple addition, it's exponential multiplication, which makes small numbers huge.

Interactions that might seem simple and linear are anything but, because everybody affects everybody else, in multiple dimensions. We acknowledge that reality with 360-Degree Evaluations, wherein everybody assesses and scores everybody else they connect with at work on key cultural principles. Then the scores for each point are added up. Results are more accurate than old-school assessments by a supervisor. Who really knows more about what it's like to work with somebody than coworkers? Who knows more about a leader, a higher-up who sees only a fraction of that leader's behavior or the people who work directly for that boss, interacting and seeing him or her in action on a daily basis?

The killer application here is using the Culture Guide as a basis for 360-Degree Evaluation, then using the results as a springboard to action. Based on assessment results, everybody creates a personal action plan to do better in areas where feedback reveals a need for improvement. The plan is presented to a supervisor, who provides input, then the team member executes the plan and improves, which will show up on the next 360-Degree Evaluation. The system shines a bright light into the human environment. There's nowhere to hide, and no wiggle room. Culture is everybody's job, not just leadership's. Your systems should reinforce that shared responsibility.

Think, Do –

❏ Add and subtract: Analyze your physical environment, and ask yourself what can be added to support your culture and what detracts from it and should be removed.

❏ Rethink your organizational dress code. Is it by design or default? Create a dress code that reflects your Culture of Success.

❏ Implement a 360-Degree Evaluation process that is driven by your Culture Guide.

9

THE LAW OF ENTROPY

NATURAL LAW:
Left to themselves, organizations inevitably fall apart and tend toward chaos.

NEVER-ENDING BATTLE

This chapter's human natural law parallels a bedrock principle of science, The Second Law Of Thermodynamics, which says that sealed-off systems tend toward a state of equilibrium, with the level of energy equalized and matter spread out in an even mix. Basically, everything just blahs out, so whatever was happening can't happen any more. Nothing can happen, ever, without some kind of outside input to create a dynamic disequilibrium – hotter here than there, more stuff on one side than the other – to get things going again. Dead blahness is entropy, considered to be a state of maximum chaos because there's no organization when everything's the same.

Our Law says, similarly, that organizations get disorganized and cease functioning properly if you don't step in and do something. But human entropy is anything but blah. It's ugly, it's a mess. Our chaos is chaotic. And messes and chaos are everywhere, lurking in the shadows and just dying to come in and undo our good work – which they'll do if we don't fight them back all day, every day. The Law of Entropy is a major force in life.

If you don't believe it, go out to the garage and think about the never-ending effort to keep things organized so there's enough room to park the car, which is the garage's intended purpose. Now and again you have to sacrifice part of a precious day off to restore order. So it goes, on a smaller scale, with clothes closets, sock drawers, junk drawers, your office, and the car. Even disciplined, compulsive neat freaks have messes sneaking up on them. Entropy follows us everywhere, all day long, and we spend a considerable amount of our time and energy fending it off. We win little victories but never defeat it, because one corrective measure is never enough.

The human body is a veritable temple to entropy. You can't brush your teeth and declare your mouth healthy and germ free. Or take a bath and enjoy the benefits long-term. Hair doesn't stay cut. A workout doesn't make you fit for life. The soul is susceptible, too, even for the devout – hence maintenance programs like daily prayer and scripture reading and religious services once a week to renew the spirit.

Cars need refueling and servicing. Roofs need to be fixed and replaced. No need to go farther, because you get the point. If humans made it or have anything to do with it, it'll go to heck and quit doing anything worthwhile if you don't keep an eye on it, take care of it, and fix what needs fixing.

YOUR TEAM IS NOT YOUR SOCK DRAWER

In the realm of the physical – machines, buildings, the body's physiology and function – entropy is a force that needs to be resisted, but there's no malign intent. A car breaks down for value-neutral mechanical reasons, not to deliberately strand you where nobody can get parts for it because the car is your enemy.

But in human interaction and behavior – the realm of workplace culture – there are enemies.

Us.

Left to ourselves, we are our own worst enemies.

With no firm direction, we will take a left turn and go straight toward negativity.

Our language reflects the truth. Approximately 70 percent of words in English that relate to emotion are negative – that's a 7 to 3 win for sad/mad/bad over glad. You can hear it in conversations in a workplace Culture by Default. Talk turns to gossip that's almost inevitably snarky, if not outright nasty. People backbite and bicker. If they're talking about bosses and work, they're complaining. The tendency is the same at the organizational level. In a power vacuum, the wrong kind of people take control for the wrong reasons, then push the wrong agenda. There are exceptions, but so rare they prove the rule. Without active oversight and encouragement to go in the right directions, people and their organizations have a tendency to go wrong. That's just how things are.

Fortunately, we are complex beings who also have better selves that want to go right, not wrong. A Culture of Success is a system to put those better selves on top, and keep them there, and kick entropy's butt – which of course does not stay kicked, so you've got to keep doing it on a daily basis, and regularly break out of your routine to have everybody do it as a team and renew commitment to the Culture of Success and each other.

If you don't make a major group effort to renew it every 90 days, your Culture of Success will, inevitably, start to fall apart.

SIGNS OF WEAR AND TEAR

Think of cultural renewal as organizational hygiene. You'll notice it's overdue, just as you notice when you don't shower for a week.

You see cracks in team cohesion, feel tension between individuals and work units. Relationships become strained, even between work friends. People don't have fun on the job and aren't functioning at peak levels because they're stressed out and worn out. These are all signs that they're forgetting why they joined the team in the first place, and the importance of the teammates who are helping them accomplish their personal and organizational goals.

TIME TO GO CAMPING

My mentor Larry Wilson, coauthor of *The One Minute Salesperson* and other books and tireless corporate trainer, has a very apt expression for off-site activities to re-bond with teammates and recommit to culture. He calls them camping experiences, and says every organization has to have one such experience on a quarterly basis. He doesn't mean that teams should literally go camping every 90 days – although a camping trip could do the job. But camping expresses the spirit of the thing – to break routine, leave the workplace, and have some sort of shared experience where workplace roles and rank-ordering don't apply, which gives everybody a chance to reconnect, and then talk about it later.

I'm in full agreement with Larry. The quarterly camping experience should be de riguer, as much a part of seriously doing business as quarterly reports and tax filings. What the experience should be is pretty much anything that gets you away from the office and puts the team together in ways unlike the usual day-in day-out routine contact.

CAMPING TIPS

I am a big fan of going off-site, because by the time the experience is really needed, people have bad associations with some of the floorspace, and by extension those who work there. To give an example: Accounting is not where you go for fun, and maybe you've had unpleasant interactions there. So you're emotionally anchored there in a negative way, and you decide you don't like the accounting work team. Stay close to where you're anchored and it will be hard to lose those emotions. But elsewhere, doing new and different things, you might remember you like some of the bean counters, and vice versa, and back in the office the bad vibe in accounting's space will be gone.

Requirements for a successful experience:

- It gets everybody out of the day-to-day routine and out of the routine brain.
- It remixes teammates in non-routine ways.
- It's not what you did last time. Experiences should be new and novel.

There's a clear "Why" and everybody understands that the point is reconnection and recommitment to each other without the normal hierarchy. Even if you're doing something silly, people need to know that this is not just a day off.

The requirements do not narrow the range of possibilities, which are nearly infinite. The following are some kinds of camping experiences that have worked for other teams and my own.

DOING GOOD

As an example of highly ambitious charity work, some of our dental clients have organized a humanitarian effort to take dentists and teams from their offices to the Dominican Republic – not just to provide free dental care, but to instill in local professionals and the community the spirit of helping.

The effort has succeeded to the point that roles have actually reversed, so now our people help the locals rather than leading them. Teams work to raise and save money for their trips, which fundamentally impacts office culture.

But you don't need to go far. Team service days to help local worthy causes, such as kitchens for the homeless, are great too. Charitable groups will be glad for the help.

LOOKING AHEAD

Being away from work doesn't mean you need to avoid the subject. A day of strategic planning – talking about your organization, setting goals and laying out new plans to reach them – can be a great, refreshing camping experience. Remember to leave the workaday mindset and hierarchy behind.

RE-ROLLOUT

This is from a team I've worked with forever that rolled out its Culture Guide 10 years ago. The leader and teammates decided to revisit their guide point by point, updating and expanding on the expectations, and recommitting to their Culture of Success.

FINE DINING

A favorite formula of mine is to take the team on a visit to another business that has absolutely nothing to do with ours and learn all we can about the ins and outs of that business and what it's like to work there. One such trip took us to a five-star restaurant here in Dallas. The executive chef arranged a behind-the-scenes tour where staffers explained how they do what they do and the inner workings of the operation, which were complicated and amazing. But the workplace culture turned out to be equally amazing. On average, team members had been there for 10 years – 10 years! – unbelievable in the notoriously high-turnover restaurant business. Leadership knew how to instill pride in their prestigious establishment and generally make everybody feel like a million bucks. Clear individual accountability and responsibility, so things were orderly and predictable, were part of the recipe, too.

For a grand finale, we enjoyed a meal together, where we talked about what we had learned that we could apply.

TRAINING DAYS

This one is dear to my heart, because teams often come to us for training, which can be a great bonding experience. On the other hand, it can be a bust. It all depends on leadership and fulfilling a couple of requirements:

A) The Why. Everybody needs to know it in advance. Though the training should cover new territory, it should also be attached to a goal that the whole team buys into and gets. And there's the big camping experience Why – reconnecting with shared vision and values and goals and, most importantly, each other.

B) Absolute, 100 percent, enthusiastic commitment by leadership, who must take part in the training as part of the team–this is not an option.

TRAINING DONE RIGHT...AND WRONG

Right – Nobody involved on this end will forget customer relations training for the bread truck drivers of a billion-dollar national bread company, who stocked store shelves and dealt with customers. The company was so big we had to schedule multiple sessions for 200 trainees apiece. On day one, we were surprised to see a roomful of top management suits, all the way up to the CEO, who asked his managers to stand if they started out driving trucks and stocking. He said to his people, "Look around. As all of you know, one of the hallmarks of success is that leadership understands what goes on in the front lines, because that's where our business succeeds." And the suits all participated in our training, beginning to end.

Wrong – This was another company, not in the bread business. At the beginning of the session, top leaders were there with the troops. The CEO gave a great rah-rah speech about how important this was for everybody. Ten minutes later we looked up and – Poof! – the CEO and big suits were gone. Halfway through the morning session, somebody raised his hand and stood up. He said he loved the training but then began to air grievances about how tough it was for him and others to live because management kept changing the formula for employee compensation in unpredictable ways. Trouble at work was clearly a bigger deal than what we were trying to teach.

Takeaways – Before they got their own training, the bread company drivers knew that all their leaders had the same experience. They got a culture-building message, loud and clear, that they're all in this together, from the top on down. People in the other company saw living proof that the CEO's words were empty, and saw top managers check out because they considered themselves special and didn't care enough to stay and share this experience like they were part of the team too. Judging by what happened, they weren't.

PLAYTIME

So long as people remember the Why, and you remix them in ways they're not used to, it's perfectly all right to go out and play together. Teams I know:

- Hiked to gorgeous waterfalls
- Went on elaborate scavenger hunts all over town
- Volunteered to clean up a church group's unused ropes course, then used it
- Ate Buffalo wings and went bowling
- Held an Office Olympics with such events as a paper plane toss and finding paperclips in a trash can full of other stuff, while blindfolded
- Learned exercises and tips on how to stay motivated from a professional fitness trainer
- Had dinner at the boss' house

VARIETY, PLANNING

Keep things interesting by changing activities, locations, mood. If you do something serious and substantive, get a little goofy next time, and vice versa.

Plan long in advance. Forward-thinking teams schedule their camping experiences a year out.

Consider divvying up the planning responsibilities between work teams, so they each have a turn to plan an experience for the whole organization.

BETWEEN CAMPING EXPERIENCES...

You still have to take steps to reinforce your Culture of Success and hold entropy at bay on a daily basis.

You hold in your hand a practical guide to doing just that. Every chapter has highly effective tactics for combating entropy. Whatever it is, if it's in this book and you haven't done it for a while, it's time to do it again.

Think, Do –

❑ Ask yourself what have been the most effective camping-like experiences for your team in the past. Why did they work?

❑ Schedule your next four camping experiences over the next 12 months. Identify the Why for each one. Assign a leader or business team to plan and carry out each one.

❑ Remember that entropy needs to be fought back constantly. Action plan all the recommendations for establishing a Culture of Success to keep yours vibrant and improving.

THE LAW OF THE INDIVISIBLE WHOLE

NATURAL LAW:
There is one real you, which ultimately is revealed.

Corollary: You cannot live a compartmentalized life.

One cannot do right in one department of life whilst he is
occupied in doing wrong in any other department.
*Life is one **indivisible whole**.*
– Mahatma Ghandi

THE LINE THAT ISN'T THERE

The natural law and Ghandi's quote, which gave the law its
name, might seem a bit personal and spiritual for a business-
oriented book like this. But it's pure, hard-nosed practicality,
especially since people have begun to work, play, and
communicate on a personal level on the internet. Problematic
postings on social media and blogs and indiscreet emails
have caused people serious problems in their professional

lives and even gotten them fired. The fastest growing areas of employment law and litigation involve drawing a line between professional and private communications, what belongs to whom, and who's accountable.

But whatever the new regulations and court rulings, for practical purposes there is no line. If you're still naïve enough to act as if you have a private life on the internet, you do so at your peril. To the world, the Off-Hours You is the Professional You. You giving a webinar is you tweeting and Instagram-ing on your smart phone, sharing pics of a crazy weekend with friends, venting about people you work with and so on. Nothing's private, and everything's forever.

One of the most rewarding programs I lead is called Eagle University (www.EagleUniversity.org), an intensive summer course for high school and college students where we teach strategies to help them gain a seven-year head start on their careers. We hammer on the need to be very careful what you do online, because people who really matter will see it. University admissions officers, scholarship committees, and employers first go to Facebook, Instagram, Twitter, and the like to pore over profiles, postings and pictures, to get a better idea about who each young person they're assessing really is. Until recently much of what they discover would have been considered personal and confidential, but not any more.

This is no longer cutting edge, of course. Social media and employment issues and the transparency of life online, whether or not transparency is desired, have been topics in the public forum for some time.

And technology did not fundamentally change the world. To be sure, the internet speeds things up and makes it easier to share thoughts and parts of your life instantly without thinking about potential consequences. But there was never as much privacy as people imagined. Today's truth – which was Mahatma Ghandi's truth – always applied: You can't be one way in one area of life, and another in another area, without spillover. If there's something wrong going on, it will catch up to you. Even if you don't get caught, you pay a heavy price for trying to compartmentalize and separate parts of your life. In the workplace, especially if you're a leader, trying to lead multiple lives causes damage to the culture. And people always know much more than you think – about you.

> The real message is not to be careful about what you say and do online – it's to be careful what you say and do, period. Whatever it is, it's the real you. You don't just own it, you're not just accountable, it's who you are. Technology just puts a spotlight on this, to remind us of what has always been true.
>
> There is one real you.

THE PRICE OF DUPLICITY

I began this book with a cautionary tale about a partner in a formerly thriving business who carried on a flagrant extramarital affair with an employee. He behaved as if he was not accountable for his actions because they happened when he was off the clock, in a private life entirely separate from professional life – or so he imagined. In fact, what he believed was nobody else's business turned out to be everybody's business, literally, because everybody in the company paid a price. The man people thought they knew – trusted partner, trusted leader – revealed by his actions that he was somebody else entirely. In their close-knit workplace team, this threw everybody off and sent trust and a sense of security straight into the dumpster. Culture turned toxic, and the clientele sensed it and began to turn away.

I know, personally, what a mess that man made of his company because I was called in to clean up and do a cultural detox. If trying to live outside Natural Law (which you can't really break) was illegal, he would have faced multiple charges of contravening more than one law and done serious time.

But even if his shameful actions stayed more or less hidden, he and others would have paid a price. Trying to lead a double life is high-stress, exhausting, and of course, high risk. It's like trying to keep double books – orders of magnitude more difficult than keeping one set in broad daylight. The time and energy expended does no one any good – least of all the duplicitous person. He deprives everybody – at work, at home, everywhere – the whole, real him, which he obviously wants to be or he wouldn't try so hard to hide behavior that belies the public persona.

> A Culture of Success is an inside job. It's a whole that is
> the sum of its human parts, and it starts within each one
> of them. Nobody's perfect. But fractured individuals who
> deliberately deceive to hide who they are can fracture the
> culture so wholeness at the team level is unattainable.

My friend, mentor, and genius rugby coach Larry Gelwix, who's
arguably the winning-est coach in sports history, says this:
"You've got to decide which team you play for. You can't have
one foot in Babylon and one foot in the Promised Land. You
can't have it both ways."

THE GLOW WITHIN

I know a member of a workplace team whose off-hours
behavior had the absolute opposite effect on her workplace
and its Culture of Success, which she strengthened. All along
she has been a valuable asset to the team and all it stands for
– diligent, hard-working, a delight just to be around. I liked her
from the first time I met her, which was years ago.

But there was one hole in this good person's life. She and
her husband were childless and were going to stay that way,
for reasons that doctors could not remedy. They began the
adoption process, which can be long and complicated as
anyone who has ever been involved in it knows. They zeroed
in on a young boy who looked like a wonderful addition to the
family. The boy was under foster care, as were the boy's two
brothers. The woman and her husband didn't know their son-

to-be had siblings until pretty late in the process. They found out, too, that the brothers were slated to be split up and go to different foster homes. The only way to keep the boys together was for an adoptive family to step up and take all three. I was not in the least surprised to learn that my friend and her husband did just that. They started wanting one child but took three, because it was the right thing to do. No surprise here either, they made a huge success of parenting the three boys.

Her teammates, who liked my friend to begin with, liked her even more.

Her off-hours self, who did a noble thing and reaped the personal rewards, was exactly the same warm, generous person they knew. Having someone like that on the team added to the spirit of the workplace. Her off-hours generosity – in direct contrast to duplicity to conceal off-hours misbehavior – built the Culture of Success.

When you're doing right and have nothing to hide, you bring your whole self to contribute to a wholesome Culture of Success.

> A decision to have a Culture of Success is a decision to be all in, not half out.

TAKE IT EVERYWHERE

At the end of our business courses, I ask this question: "How many of you feel that you will be a better person at home and in your personal relationships because of things you just learned to do at the office?"

After the question, I look out into a sea of raised hands.

Why? Because the reality is that you cannot improve in one area of life without improving in every other area. This is the upside of wholeness. Live the Culture of Success, using principles laid out in this book, and it will positively impact your whole life.

In this book we have introduced 10 Natural Laws that are foundational to a Culture of Success, along with related ideas that allow you to build on those Natural Laws. These laws and systems apply to one person as much as they do to an organization. So it all starts with you. My personal challenge to you is to:

- Learn the Natural Laws
- Put them to work for you by applying the systems in this book
- Positively impact every culture in which you are involved

And when you do, you will have impact, because you are the Culture of Success.

ABOUT THE AUTHOR:

Steven J. Anderson is an entrepreneur, author, presenter and agent for creating a *Culture of Success*. You can find him at www.StevenJAnderson.com

Every culture is made of up more than one person. Here are just a few examples of cultures he has co-created with others that you can tap into to add to your own *Culture of Success*.

Crown Council - www.CrownCouncil.com - Creating a Culture of Success in Your Practice. The home for top dental practices that are committed to an ongoing, never-ending process of improving and delivering exceptional clinical care and patient service in a *Culture of Success*. For information call: 1-800-CROWN-58 or log onto www.CrownCouncil.info

Total Patient Service Institute - www.TotalPatientSerice.com - Team specific training, live seminars, and in-office coaching for creating a *Culture of Success*.

Smiles for Life Foundation – Dentistry's leading cause-related campaign having raised over $30 million for children's charitable causes world-wide. Discover how you can participate as a patient or a practice by logging onto www.SmilesForLife.org.

Eagle University – www.EagleUniversity.org - Youth leadership training helping high school and college age students get a 7 year head start on their career. Week long Eagle U courses give students the secrets, skills, and strategies to advance their careers and their lives beyond the ordinary.

I APPRECIATE...

It takes a team to create a *Culture of Success*. I am fortunate to be surrounded by great teams who work daily to create great cultures and have a positive influence on those with whom they work and serve.

I appreciate

The Crown Council Team

Because

Lead by Greg Anderson who continues to be
a great brother and business partner for over
34 years and Stuart Anderson who help dental
professionals create and maintain
a Culture of Success in their practices
and their lives.

I appreciate

The Total Patient Service Institute team

Because

Many team members have worked together
for over a decade to customize Culture of Success
solutions for practices including Brenda Turner,
Pam Peterson, Chris Toconis, Maribeth Brown,
Tanya Bailey, Aaron Ganir, Shana Ackerman,
Lameka weeks, Janet Powe, JC Meves, Steve Bastain
and a growing team that continues to expand.

I appreciate

The Eagle U Team of Volunteers

Because

Lead by Maria Grasso that donates time
and wisdom for the benefit of high school
and college students to help them get a
7 year head start on their career.

I appreciate

The teams on our most recent creations

Because

Lead by Parker Ence at Dental Warranty Corp.
and Ryan Moore at Capstone Dental
who exemplify creating a Culture of Success
from the ground up.

I appreciate

Mike Steere

Because

The man who makes the words come to life
on the printed page from our very first
work together over twenty years ago.
Thanks for putting the Culture of Success in
understandable, readable, printed form.

I appreciate

Art and Jan Anderson (Dad and Mom)

Because

You have instilled a Culture of Success
in 7 children and a never ending line of posterity.

Thanks again Dad for that ticket!

I appreciate

Ashlin, Abby, Erin, Emily, Olivia, Avery and Owen

Because

These awesome kids encourage and
pray for their dad every day
that he will be successful.

I appreciate

Cheryl

Because

You're my biggest cheerleader
and love of my life
who has believed in me for over twenty years.
I hope it continues to be better
than you thought it would be!

I appreciate

My Heavenly Father

Because

The originator of every Natural Law
and true author of
the Culture of Success.

I appreciate

you

Because

You have taken the time to read, think
and do what is suggested in this book.
All my best in your continual, never ending efforts to
create a Culture of Success.

Steve